NOTES ON GENESIS.

NOTES ON GENESIS

BY THE LATE

FREDERICK W. ROBERTSON, M.A.

OF BRIGHTON

NEW EDITION

LONDON

KEGAN PAUL, TRENCH, TRÜBNER & CO. Ltd.

DRYDEN HOUSE, GERRARD STREET, W.

1906

PREFACE.

—◆◆◆—

THE incomplete and fragmentary character of the following notes has delayed their appearance in their present shape, and has caused me to hesitate long as to the expediency of publishing them. But the reception already accorded to my father's writings has been such as to confirm my own conviction that any authentic record of his thoughts possesses an intrinsic interest and value transcending the mere form in which they are clothed; and I believe that the "Notes on Genesis" will not be found deficient in those qualities which mark the works already published.

As to the circumstances under which the Lectures were delivered, of which these are the rough notes, but few words of explanation seem necessary. That they were not undertaken until after long and systematic preparation a reference to my father's letters will clearly show. For the rest, no better plan, I think, can be pursued than to quote the following passage from the "Life" by Mr. Stopford Brooke.

"In January, 1850, Mr. Robertson went away to recruit his health. On his return he commenced lecturing in the afternoons on the Book of Genesis. He met the difficulties of the earlier chapters with mingled wisdom and freedom; he fairly stated the claims of scientific and historical truth, even when they were in conflict with the narrative of the sacred text; and, while declaring that the Mosaic cosmogony could not be reconciled with geological facts, still succeeded in showing its inner harmony, in principles, with the principles of scientific geology. Neither did he shrink from putting his congregation in possession of the results of German criticism upon Genesis. He made them acquainted with the discussion on the Jehovah and Elohim documents, but he did not deny the Mosaic compilation of these documents. He discussed fully the question of the universality of the Flood. He spoke with a boldness, adorned with a rare reverence, upon the vexed and generally avoided subjects of the confusion of tongues, the destruction of the cities of the plain, the temptation of Abraham. In no case, however, was his preaching destructive, but constructive. Men went away from his chapel opposed, it is true, to the popular theory of Inspiration, but deeply convinced of *an* inspiration. It was, indeed, impossible, in treating of these matters to avoid the great question of Inspiration and its limits. It was therefore introduced incidentally from Sunday to Sunday."

CHARLES BOYD ROBERTSON.

LONDON: *November*, 1876.

CONTENTS.

—◆◆—

CONTENTS.

NOTES ON GENESIS.

LECTURE I.

Sunday Afternoon, February 17, 1850.

GENESIS i. 1–3.

WE began two years ago the practice of giving the Sunday morning to a sermon, and the afternoon to a lecture. And the difference between the two was that in the morning we took for our subject some single text and endeavoured to exhaust it ; but in the afternoon a chapter, and endeavoured to expound the general truths which were contained therein. The sermon was hortatory and practical ; the lecture was didactic. The first appealed rather to the heart and to the conscience ; the second rather to the intellect and the analytic faculty. In this way we have already considered in a series of lectures the Books of Samuel and the Acts of the Apostles. The book for exposition during the ensuing year is the Book of Genesis.

The Book of Genesis may be ranged under two great divisions, the point of separation being found at the end of the eleventh chapter. The first division gives the history of the

B

creation and first ages of the world; the last that of Abraham
and his descendants.   The first is a history not so much of the
Jews alone as of the whole human race.   It belongs to a time
when the Jews were not yet a nation.   We are told of the
world as it was before the time of Abraham; and we are
taught that the individuals then living had dealings with God.
We are told of Adam who heard His voice in the garden, and
Enoch who walked with Him; and all this assures our hearts
that God did not leave the world without any revelation save
that given to the Jews; that on the contrary each individual
had a revelation given him; and that consequently each will be
judged according to the light he has received.

Upon this first section of Genesis then we make to-day a few
preliminary remarks.

I. Of the creation two accounts are here given.   The first
begins in the first chapter and extends to the third verse of the
second; the second account occupies the rest of the second
chapter: and these two accounts differ from one another in
some particulars.   Every one who is familiar with the phraseology of Scripture knows that the language in the opening of the
second account, " These are the generations of the heavens and
of the earth, when they were created " (chap. ii. 4), indicates a
change of subject; so that we are led to conclude that the one
account is supplemental to the other.   In the first we are told of
God as a creator; in the second, of God as a moral governor.
In the first the name brought forward is God (Elohim) simply,
in the second it is the Lord God, *i.e.* Jehovah Elohim.   In the
first we have simply a history of man's creation; in the second
his moral history, the creation of both male and female, and

the institution of marriage. In the second we have some things added; but in the first the gradations in which things were created. In the first we have the rest, the sabbath rest of God; in the second it is not mentioned. So that it would appear that Moses was inspired by God to make this second account supplemental to the other, and that, properly speaking, we have only one.

II. We remark again that the accounts given of God in this section of Genesis represent Him as a creator. In those early times there was a vast amount of atheism. How the world came into being was a question to all. Some spoke of atoms having certain powers to unite, whilst others represented that the world was Divine, but that there was no God, no spirit. In opposition to these and other views, Moses, inspired by the Divine Mind, came forward and declared the everlasting distinction between the creation and the Creator, between the creature and Him who formed it. The heavens were not God, the planets and stars were not God; they merely came from the hand of God. Therefore we are taught here a most important truth, the personality of God. Now for personality we should say that there were necessary three things, self consciousness, will, character. You may have self consciousness, and yet not be a person. Suppose the lake on which the sky is reflected were self conscious but incapable of moving, it would have no personality. Suppose a living thing with self consciousness and choice, and nothing more, you will there only have got an animal; it would have self consciousness and will, but not character. Therefore Moses tells us that God created the world in the first place in His self consciousness, "in the beginning God created the heaven and the earth"; in the second place by will, for He said "Let there be light"; in the third place filling it, as He created it, with His character, for the Lord looked upon His world "and behold it was very good." In other words, he tells the personality of God.

III. Again we remark on the Divine origin of order. Before the creation of the world all was chaos, darkness moved on tne face of the waters; but with creation order began: and if we look over this world of God's we shall see that all is order therein. It may be that when we look on cultivated land we think order man's production, disorder God's. When the garden or the field has been once cultivated and then passes to a state of nature, it appears chaotic to us, for we have seen it otherwise; but in the vast tracts of country untouched by human art all is order and regularity for miles and hundreds of miles. Nature is always at rest in its order, and God is in its order. When we look on it we know that there is no state in the soul of man more undivine, more ungodly, than disorder or confusion. Nothing less resembles the mind of God than the mind of him who kneels down to pray with troubled worldly thoughts. Order within the soul is the will of God, and the soul that has it resembles the Divine creation.

IV. Again we observe the gradations of things made. We are told that God proceeded from the less perfect to the more perfect: first inorganic life, after that the vegetable, then the animal, and then by degrees man, made in the image of his Creator. We find the same principle in all that God does now: in the passage of the caterpillar into the chrysalis and then into the butterfly we have the image of God's continual method of work. It is a method we find in our own life: we find first of all the mere animal existence, then the development of the intellect, the thinking being, then the bringing out of the conscience, and then the Spirit of God working out the formation of the spiritual man. There is something in all this that speaks to us of the slow progress of the mind. It is a marvellous thing to look at human life, to mark the number of years spent in mere animal existence, and then to see that mind appears just for a few years in later life. But slow as the progress is, it is progress. We are made conscious of God's law, and the lesson we learn is that the man who is not advancing is directly reversing the order of God.

V. We remark again that, next to the work of creation, the first Divine motion was the creation of light: "Let there be light" God said, "and there was light." God spoke His will, and the heavens were made, He gave the word and they were created. Man may tell us of the development of the world from the theistical or atheistical point of view, but the simplest and most religious way is to look at this world as the expression of the will of God. It is sufficient if we feel that the light reveals to us something of the will of the Eternal; enough if the beauty of nature can speak to us of the mind of God; if the blue heaven above and the green earth below tell of our Father's home; if day and night, light and darkness are symbols of the word God has spoken out of Himself in the creation of the world. The ancients, seeing this Divine origin of light, worshipped the sun and moon and hosts of heaven; but they went too far in this direction. They isolated light as

alone Divine. Light standing as the symbol of all things
Divine, darkness became to them the symbol of the contrary. Light was the realm in which God ruled. But this
was only half a truth, God created darkness as well as light,
and is as much a ruler of the darkness as of the light.
Darkness is given to us for repose. Man spends his days
in labour, in the fever of getting and spending; but when
the shades of evening close in and the stars come out to keep
their quiet watch over the earth, man looking upwards sees in
the stars and the peace of night an emblem of the deep repose
of God, and his heart is kindled into adoration. With no less
truth than beauty has it been said that the touch of darkness
produces worship in the soul of man; that the broad band
which goes round the planet influences men, so that when
darkness is disappearing before the light, and light before the
darkness, men kneel down to worship, as if only in twilight and
darkness man could worship God. In the withdrawal of light
we have a revelation higher almost than that given us in light.

VI. Once more we have to make a preliminary remark.
There are men who look into this book, expecting it to teach
them all the truth respecting God's creation; but they find
that the records God has given in nature, drawn out and
systematised in the science of geology, cannot cohere with
the account of Moses. Upon this there have been two or
three modes of evasion tried: first that of those who refused
to recognise at all what this science taught; secondly, that
of those who, by spreading the six days of creation over an un-
limited surface, and making them represent any space of time,
would have compromised the matter; the third and I believe

the last expedient is to allow a chasm between the first and second verses, between which time is given for all that geology requires. But we need not resort to methods such as these. There are two revelations : one God has written on the page of creation, to be ascertained by investigation, and it is just as inspired, just as true, just as much to be received as God's word as the handwriting on the wall of Babylon ; the other revelation is written in the page of Scripture. The first belongs to physical phenomena, the second to the spiritual dealings of God with man. For instance we are told that God created the firmament, and placed it between the waters above and the waters below. The account tells, in accordance with the knowledge of the time, what the firmament then seemed to men ; it does not pretend to state what it actually is. It uses the language of the day ; and if God had a revelation to make now, it would be given in the expression of the day : it would say "the sun rises," though that is not scientifically correct. But this inconsistency with physical truth does not invalidate the great broad spiritual truths which revelation is meant to teach. Does it alter or weaken the spiritual facts revealed in this account of creation: that God does all by degrees, that He is the moral governor of the world ; the spiritual truth that the introduction of a sinful will produces immense gain in point of knowledge and immense loss in point of purity ; that the man who has done wrong feels naked and ashamed in the sight of God ?

And now, my brethren, in conclusion, we are at the commencement of a new book. There is something solemn in a commencement, because it reminds us of a close. Twice have I begun and twice have I finished a book here. Twice have I reminded you that many present at the beginning of my lectures would never live to hear their termination. Again and again has that prediction been fulfilled. The young, the vigorous, the beautiful, have been taken away; and many of us who expected our summons are listening still. But do not forget that there are those among us now who will not hear this course of lectures close. Brother men, as we look back into those far distant reaches of the past and speak of cities and peoples long ago perished, should we not be reminded that life is but a span? May God grant me courage, perseverance, boldness, inward strength to ascertain the truth and teach it! May God give my hearers the heart to attend with teachableness, and with the love which covereth all things, even a multitude of sins!

LECTURE II.

Sunday Afternoon, March 3, 1850.

GENESIS i. 26–31.

THE subject of our exposition to-day will be confined to the account which is given of the creation on the sixth day. First however we shall recapitulate the spiritual truths at which we have already arrived. The Mosaic account then of the creation established these principles : 1. That the universe as it exists now is different from the universe as it existed once ; in other words, things are not as they were. 2. That the creation of the world was not the work of many gods but of One. 3. That it was a Person that effected this vast work, and not some law of the universe gradually educing all things from a power that was inherent in matter. 4. Respecting the character of the Creator the Israelite was taught that He had formed all things good ; and here we have the foundation of all morality, the eternal difference between right and wrong which existed in God before the world was, which God could never change, and in obedience to which He created all things, for He beheld His universe and pronounced it very good. 5. The Israelite was taught also the divinity of order. God was represented as evolving harmony from discord, as repressing the unruly elements and bringing them into obedience. And herein men were taught the Divine character of order ; that it is the law of man's existence ; that the unregu-

lated or unruly heart 'is like the ship with an insubordinate
crew which is wrecked on the ocean ; that order is to pervade
the church, to rule the state, to regulate the family, to influence man's personal happiness, his affections, his desires.
6. The Israelite was taught also this : that it was gradation that
regulated God's creation, to be traced not only in this that the
more perfect forms of life were created last, but also in the fact
that more work was done at the close than at the beginning of
the creative period.   We are told that God did almost nothing
on the second day, except the separation of the waters which
were above from the waters which were below the earth, but on
the sixth all the animals were created and man the top and
crown of all things.   And this is true of every work which will
stand the test of time.   It must not be hastily done, but
thoughtfully planned and carried out with steady and increasing
energy. God who works for eternity lays His foundations deep,
He does not extemporize. It matters not whether it be in things
great or small : quick, mere outside work is done for time ; meant
for show, it falls speedily to nothing, there is in it nothing
belonging to eternity. If then a man would follow God he
must be content to toil and toil to the last. 7. Once more,
the principle of the providence of the Almighty emerges from
the history of the creation.   We read of man's creation and
the creation of the beasts.   The vegetables He did not create
till the earth was dry ; the animals not till the vegetables were
prepared for their sustenance ; and man not till the kingdom
was put in order which man should rule.   Now this is what
we call providence in God, foresight or prudence in man.
Thus we see how a mere earthly virtue may in another sense be

a spiritual excellence, and it is the duty of man to rise into this higher view. The bird, taught by God its instinct, produces the nest before there are young to live in it. The animal too can provide for its wants ; but when we come to man we should find these earthly virtues rising almost into Divine attributes, we should feel that the loss of them is a violation of the moral law. The man for instance, who without any control over his passions, any regulation of his will, has brought a family into this world without the means to provide for them is not to be looked upon merely as one who has erred against worldly prudence, but as one who has sinned against the law of the universe, who has committed a moral fault. The religious society which prepares for itself a sphere larger than it can manage, and then has the effrontery to tell us that such imprudence is Christian faith and zeal instead of neglect, has sinned against not merely common prudence but Divine law. It is these spiritual truths that we extract from the doctrine of this chapter.

Lastly, we have before endeavoured to show the real nature and inspiration of Genesis. We have not tried to make Moses' writings agree with the present state of science and knowledge. Moses had not a scientific message to deliver ; but the marvel is this, that there is not one spiritual fact that can be overturned. The cosmogony of the Phœnicians was atheistical ; so was that of the Egyptians ; in North America the Indians have a cosmogony not atheistical but simply ludicrous. Now comes the question, how is it that out of all these cosmogonies one only is found that stands the test of great scientific principles ?

Science declares that the God of the universe is a God of order, that there has been gradation in the growth of the world, that there is unity at the root of variety. Moses declares so also in the simple childlike language of those days before science had existed.

We pass on now to the chief work of creation on the sixth day, the creation of mankind. We are told that the language in which that creation is spoken of, *i.e.* "Let *us* make man," implies the doctrine of a plurality of persons in the Deity; in other words, Moses, whose avowed object it was to teach the unity of God, so far forgot himself as to teach the contrary. We are told again that we are to found on this account the doctrine of the Trinity. There is no reason, only ignorance, in such a view. The Hebrew when he wanted to speak of anything majestic spoke in the plural, not in the singular. He spoke of "heavens" not of heaven. In the same way he spoke of Gods, yet meaning only One. Exactly in the same way the courtesy of modern ages has substituted "you" for "thou"; and here the very form of the writer's language required that he should put "us" instead of "me" in speaking of the majesty of God. Further, to look for the Trinity here would be utterly to reverse the whole method of God's revelation. We know from our own lives that God does things gradually, and we conclude that He did the same with His chosen people. He had to teach them first the unity of the Godhead; the nature of that unity was to be taught afterwards. Conceive what would have been the result in an age of polytheism of teaching the Trinity. The doctrine would have inevitably degenerated into tritheism. To how many is the blessed doctrine of the Trinity only tritheism now, nay more, many pass it over altogether; and if there are now but few to whom it is a doctrine of spiritual comfort, could there have been any had the truth been revealed by Moses?

With respect to man himself we are told on the one side that he is dust, "formed of the dust of the earth." The phrase marks our affinity to the lower animals. It is a humbling thing to see how little different the form of man's skeleton is from that of the lower animals; more humbling still when we compare their inward physiological constitution with our own. Herein man is united to the beasts. But "God breathed into man's nostrils the breath of life": herein he is united to the Deity. The heathen, recognising in their own way the spiritual in man, tried to bridge over the chasm between it and the earthly by making God more human. The way of revelation on the contrary is to make man more godlike, to tell of the Divine idea yet to be realized in his nature. Nor have we far to go to find some of the traces of this Divine in human nature. 1. We are told that God is just and pure and holy. What is the meaning of these words? Speak to the deaf man of hearing, or the blind of light, he knows not what you mean. And so to talk of God as good and just and pure implies that there is goodness, justice, purity, within the mind of man. 2. We find in man the sense of the infinite: just as truly as God is boundless is the soul of man boundless; there is something boundless, infinite, in the sense of justice, in the sense of truth, in the power of self sacrifice. 3. In man's creative power there is a resemblance to God. He has filled the world with his creations. It is his special privilege to subdue the powers of nature to himself. He has forced the lightning to be his messenger, has put a girdle round the earth, has climbed up to the clouds and penetrated down to the depths of the sea. He has turned the forces of nature against herself; commanding the winds to help him in braving the sea. And marvellous as is man's rule over external, dead nature, more marvellous still is his rule over animated nature. To see the trained falcon strike down the quarry at the feet of his master, and come back, when God's free heaven is before him; to see the hound use his speed in the service of his master, to take a prey not to be given to himself; to see the camel of the desert carrying man through his own home : all these show the creative power of man and his resemblance to God the creator. 4. Once more, God is a God of order. The universe in which God reigns is a domain in which order reigns from first to last, in which everything has its place, its appointed position; and the law of man's life, as we have seen, is also order.

But in the case of man two mistakes are possible. The man of unruly passions may say, God endowed me with these inclinations, I have a right to obey them. I answer thus : It is true, man cannot have a higher rule of life than this, to live according to his nature ; but the question is, What is the whole nature of man ? The mainspring is a most important portion of the watch; but will it, unregulated, fulfil the watch's object? Man gives way to his passions, and says, I am living according to my nature. Brother men, is your nature then the nature of the beasts ? have you no higher nature than that ?

The next mistake is made when spirituality is over regarded ; when it is supposed that a man is to live some imaginary life above all the lower passions. The perfect nature, the true order of man's life, is when the two are harmonised and one made superior to the other, when the flesh is subdued to the spirit and the spirit rules. We need not entrance ourselves into devotion; we need not give ourselves up to fasting. It is not a morbid way of looking upon our nature that God requires. These lower feelings become sublime, not by being crushed, but by being subdued to the spirit and made its instruments. For instance, many have thought that there is nothing more humiliating than eating and drinking; but when we go to the labourer's cottage and watch the wife engaged in the preparation of her husband's meal we feel that these exertions have been ennobled by their object, for they are made the channel of a holy love; nay, we have the highest authority to say that a cup of cold water given in love to a thirsty man tends to the elevation of our lower nature. My Christian brethren, the question which is every moment determining itself is this, whether we are rising in spiritual excellence, or sinking to the level of the brutes that perish; whether anarchy or the true order reigns in us.

LECTURE III.

Sunday Afternoon, March 10, 1850.

"These are the generations of the heavens and of the earth when they
were created, in the day that the Lord God made the earth and the heavens."
—GENESIS ii. 4.

THE first account of the creation concluded with a circumstance which we had not time to expound, the
sabbath rest of God when all the earth was complete. We
are told, God rested on the seventh day from all His works;
in which we are to guard ourselves from attributing too literal
a meaning to the expression used. We are not to understand
that God ceased from creation, for creation is going on every
day. Nature is God at work, and, speaking humanly, just as
the work of nature seems to be accomplished when winter becomes spring, when old passes into new; so, when Chaos took
form and order, and beauty and harmony had been established,
God seemed to be at rest. And this expression, the Rest of
God, is not used singularly here. When we say that God
was angry, God repented, we use a similar language. But
though creation ceased not, from that moment new creations
ceased. The forms and types then established became the
models according to which God has been creating ever since.
This is the rest of God, the Sabbath of the Everlasting.

Our next question is, what did this statement mean to the
Israelites? We find that whatever Divine commands Moses
gave the Israelites, he communicated to them their grounds.

If he required them to believe in the unity of God he gave them an historical revelation that this same God had been believed in by their fathers. If he commanded them to take Canaan he told them their fathers had possessed it, and that its present possessors were usurpers and interlopers. In the same way when he gave them the law of the Jewish sabbath he gave them along with it its basis, that is, the revelation of God's Sabbath. At the time of the Israelitish captivity in Egypt we find not a trace of the sabbath. It was a new thing when Moses gave it by God's command as a law unto the Israelites ; and he made it the seal of a covenant which marked them out from other nations. On what did it rest? It rested upon something greater than mere human will, or even Divine will, and that something was an eternal necessity of man's nature, derived from a similar necessity in the nature of his Maker. And this is the only ground on which *our* obligation to keep the sabbath day can rest. We cannot place it on the ground of the Mosaic law.

We have abrogated almost all that belonged to the sabbath day. We have taken away "every manner of work." We have changed many other important particulars. From sunset to sunset we have altered to from midnight to midnight. And then, instead of "the seventh day," we have left only this "one day in seven"; and the sceptical mind requirest some proof of the moral obligation of keeping one day without work when we have admitted all the rest of the covenant to be ceremonial. We must take higher ground, and tell the doubter that there is an eternal necessity for the recurring

c

sabbath. It is just on this, only on this perpetual necessity of a sabbath, that our observance of the sabbath must be founded, in this requirement of physical rest by our nature, in the fact also that it is only by means of these stated returns of particular seasons that man can, in rest from temporal concerns, fix his attention on his Maker.

There is a further necessity for a similar outward form in the mode of worship on the sabbath, which illustrates the primal necessity of having a day set apart. Thoughtful men have often asked why they cannot go out and have their worship in the great temple of the universe. The man who argues so knows not his own nature. There is a temple of God's universe, and those who deny it forget a grand and spiritual truth ; but the feeling gained in this temple of God is one thing, that gained in the church of God is another. We may in like manner worship God all the week, but the emotion of worship on the sabbath when we lay aside work is different from the emotions felt towards God in the midst of work.

At the same time the mode of observing the sabbath must manifestly vary according to the age of the individual, according to the place where he lives, and the age of the world in which he lives. That rest which is fit for the old is not fit for the young; that which suits the intellectual does not suit the unlearned. The man who has strained his intellect all the week, can we not understand that if he took his spade and indulged in mental relaxation for two hours whilst digging in his garden, he would be observing the sabbath? There is a difference also in the kind of rest made by national custom and by ranks and by occupation; that which will do for the rich man will not do for the poor; that which will do for the Jew will not do for the Christian. The stern old Jewish sabbath is extremely difficult for one of us to comprehend. We know indeed that national habits make a difference when we compare what the Jew and the Englishman thinks sabbatical rest to be. Conceive a man making the sabbath day a day of absolute rest, going so far as to permit no music, take no walk, enjoy no relaxation, thrown on himself; and yet such was the manner in which the Jewish sabbath was kept. And it was this difference from our more easy and lax modern manners that made the Israelites the spiritual teachers of the world. They were the least accustomed of all nations to abstract thought, and yet it was this stern rule which made such men as Moses, Paul, and David.

We pass on now to the second account of the creation. It is, observe, a second account, not a continuation of the first.

The writing tells of a different age; it speaks of a different composer. And the very superscription is the recognised mode of language used to indicate a change of subject. Evidently this account goes back on the last. At the end of the first, all was created: at the beginning of the second, man is not made, nor are the beasts. We find very important differences between these two accounts; for example, in their history of the creation of man, male and female. In the first the order of man's creation is narrated; in the second, his spiritual history. In the first, God is a creator; in the second, God is the moral governor of the universe. Yet let us not suppose for one moment that these are two separate accounts thrown together with no object. They are manifestly linked together, each is supplemental to the other. In the first, we have these spiritual truths—the unity of God, His personality, His order : in the second, His dealings with nature and with the mind of man. God gives man law, and annexes to his obedience and disobedience reward and punishment.

We make three remarks on this second account. The first is with reference to the reason given for man's creation, that there was a man wanted to till the ground. We should not have said that of man. We should have held another view, and looked upon ourselves as the rulers of this world for whom all things were created, were it not for this verse which teaches us the truth. In the order of creation man is the highest ; but the object for which man is created is that he should, like all the rest, minister to the advance of all things. *That* is our position here ; we are here to do the world's work.

The next thing we have to observe is the unity of the human race. On this point we do not decide dogmatically, nor take it for granted that it is distinctly revealed that there was only one pair of the human race, if science can prove that there were several pairs created instead of one. All that we are told in the first account is that God, in the beginning, created them male and female. All that we are told in the second is that He placed Adam and Eve in paradise. Theologically, the unity of the human race is of great importance. There was a time when scientific men believed the human race must have been derived from different parents. They saw so great a difference in races of men that they tried to prove the Bible account untrue. It seems to me, however, that science now compels us to pronounce that the human race must have had a single origin. The differences of race which seem insuperable on the supposition of one origin vanish by change of mental culture and of climate; and the wisest philosophers have come to this conclusion, that there is no reason why the most degraded of the human species should not have come from the same stock as the most polished Europeans. This question derives its interest from the importance of the doctrine of the equality of the human race. That doctrine has no doubt been misused and perverted, so that there is a prejudice against it and against him who dares to believe in the equality of man. We do not mean to say that men are all spiritually or intellectually equal; much less do we mean to say that the way to find the truest and wisest senators to rule the land is by giving every man the power of voting; but we mean by equality that there is no eternal difference between men. Between the highest and the lowest animals there is an everlasting difference, but none between the highest and lowest men; and it is only as this is realized that we can ever feel the existence of our common humanity in Jesus Christ. Nor is history a silent witness of this truth. The descendants of the wild tribes who in former ages invaded these shores in their war ships are now ruling these civilized realms of ours. On the other hand, Greece, once mistress of arts, is now bereft of her ancient perception of beauty; and Rome, once the iron kingdom, lies like a wreck upon the ocean of this world. In these changes produced by time we have a sort of proof of the equality of men.

The next thing to observe is this, that we have here a hint respecting immortality. It must have struck every attentive reader of the Scriptures, that in the Old Testament there is so little allusion to futurity. That it was a matter of doubt we learn from this fact, that when the Redeemer came to this world it was a question whether the sacred writings did predict a resurrection or not. It was held moreover as a speculation by one of the most gigantic minds of the age just past, —by Warburton,—that the Divine legation of Moses was proved by the fact that the Israelites received it though he sought their submission by no promise of future rewards, by no threats of future punishment. This tells of the exceeding faintness with which that doctrine must be spoken of in the Pentateuch, if spoken of at all. And here we come into apparent contradiction with the Church of England ; for the Seventh Article declares " that both in the Old and New Testament everlasting life is offered to mankind by Christ. Wherefore they are not to be heard which feign that the old fathers did look only for transitory promises."

Now, if we can reconcile these two things we shall be able to understand and get a deep glance into God's revelation of futurity. You will not find in the Old Testament a decided revelation of the life to come, but you will catch there many glimpses from which such a doctrine might have been elaborated. When God speaks of Himself as the God of Abraham, Isaac, and Jacob, there is apparently in such a passage no mention of the life to come ; yet from it Christ derived this most important truth, that God is not the God of the dead but of the *living*, the Everlasting is He to whom they *live* still. Just such is the hint we find in this second chapter of Genesis. We are told in a phrase that declares the dignity of man's nature that God breathed into his nostrils the breath of life. And when the mind of the Israelite began to brood on this he would remember that there was also a sad, dark intimation, "Dust thou art, and unto dust thou shalt return," apparently a denial of immortality. But then there were aspirations in the soul that never could be quenched; and this yearning aspiration would bring him back again to ask : "Dust is not all; the breath of God, what has become of that?" And that he would argue thus, my Christian brethren, is by no means a fancy; the phrases excite thought, they direct it in a certain manner; they are vague, but they have an aim. And comparing them with our higher knowledge we understand that God's revelation is made in this gradual way; that slight hints of a truth are first given, and that then it is defined more and more clearly.

LECTURE IV.

Sunday Afternoon, March 31, 1850.

GENESIS iii.

WE have contemplated man in the state of innocence, that bright and blessed condition represented as the garden state : a state in which he had everything which belonged to domestic happiness, in which the earth itself was one great garden, every flower his to pluck, every fruit to taste; his life was a life of blessedness and rest with God. But now the scene changes. Over all has come a dark, dense cloud, a shadow of sadness, the shadow of death. The garden state is no longer his state, this world is no longer paradise, it has become earth. There are in it thorns and briers; its sweets must be extracted by toil and anguish. This is the penalty of sin, of man's first disobedience, of the crime which showed his heart was not altogether right with God. There is however this difference between criminality and sinfulness. Criminality is the transgression of a law, sinfulness is want of harmony of mind, not necessarily a state in which man is committing actual offences, but one in which the heart is no longer in harmony with the universe ; and this sinfulness is an extinction of original nobleness. With a deep significance was it written that there was a flaming sword forbidding man's return to Eden; for it manifestly implies that there were longings, a desire to go back. Nay there is a feeling in every one of us, more or less, till the gospel of Christ has in all its power and strength enabled us to rise to holiness, that the earth is not what it was ; that a glory has passed away, that the innocence of childhood is gone, that there is none of us who is what he might have been, that life and its temptations have acted injuriously upon a spirit originally created and destined for union with God.

We shall consider first the moral and then the penal results of the fall.

I. Its moral results.

They are those which tell upon the character or inward being of a man, those which are exerted from within a man's own constitution ; the penal, those which are executed on him from without. In murder the penal consequence is the destruction of life upon the scaffold ; the moral, the injury that is done to a man's inward constitution, the remorse, the hardness, the degradation of character which he endures. Of these moral consequences there is (1) Separation from nature. This we find in the verse "they knew that they were naked" (ver. 7). The deep spiritual meaning here is that it is not possible for a man to sin without becoming thereby separated from nature. Things naturally innocent and pure become tainted by sin. The worst misery a man can bring on himself by sin is that those things which to pure minds bring nothing but enjoyment are turned for him into fuel for evil lusts and passions, and light the flames of hell within his soul. And such a difference there is between the things we call modesty and prudery. In modesty things are passed over which to others are impure ; but in prudery there is a prurient love of evil, so that those things are reckoned evil which have in them nothing that is impure.

Another of these moral consequences is separation from God. Adam and his wife heard the voice of the Lord God walking in the garden in the cool of the day; and they hid themselves from His presence, for they were afraid. We have in this an account adapted to oriental nations, for in eastern countries it is customary to walk out in the evening to catch the fresh breeze. We are told that God did this, that is, a human feeling is attributed to God. Let the sceptic enjoy his merriment. To us there is something most touching in the statement that to our first parents in the most hallowed hour of the whole day the voice of God seemed like the thundering of the Divine anger. A child might interpret that rightly to himself. When he has done wrong he is afraid, he dares not hear a sound; a common noise, in the trembling insecurity in which he lives, seems to him God's voice of thunder. To the apostles the earthquake at Philippi was a promise of release from prison; to the sinful jailer a thing of judgment and wrath: "Sirs, what shall I do to be saved?"

And here I interrupt myself for a moment that we may remind ourselves of one of those things which whenever they take place require to be brought before the congregation. One of our members since last Sunday has heard this voice in the coolness of the evening. He had told me not three hours before of his anticipations of that voice, and that he was expecting a gradual extinction of his sight. Within three hours the summons came and he was in a state of entire unconsciousness. Since then his voice has been heard once in the monosyllable "Pray," once in thanks for some service rendered him; twice has he grasped my hand convulsively with a deep look of gratitude as I knelt beside his bed in prayer. The summons was given him, he was not afraid. To those now enjoying life I would say, Or ever the silver cord be loosed and the golden bowl broken, and the seal of the eternal stamped on you for ever, dare you meet your God? dare you hear His voice?

The third of these moral consequences of sin is selfishness. The culprits are occupied entirely with their own hearts; each denies the guilt which belongs to each; each throws the blame upon the other; Adam says it was Eve, Eve that it was the serpent. And this is the very central principle of sin : properly speaking there is no other sin but selfishness. The agriculturist distinguishes between two sorts of roots: those which go deep down into the ground without dividing; and those which divide off into endless fibrils and shoots. Selfishness is like the latter kind; it is the great root of sin from which others branch out. It produced in our first parents falsehood; and all transgression, if we look but rightly at it, is falsehood. If the mason's work will not stand, it is false to the universe; if a man does not succeed in what he undertakes, he is false. It produced in them also cowardice. We talk with contempt of mere animal courage : yet there is in it an unselfishness, it may be, a reckless fearlessness; it is at least the pursuit of something higher than pleasure, and looked at rightly, all goodness is courage. What is purity but the bravely bidding away from the mind all that can destroy the soul? What is truth but the daring of all consequences; the truth, which will not merely be true when falsehood is unnecessary, but which is true under all circumstances? What again is persevering goodness in anything but this brave unruffled power of saying again and again to any interruption the unswerving No, and not a wavering Yes? And, my brethren, there is one special way in which this shows itself, a daring to acknowledge that we have done wrong. There is indeed a daring which will rise in physical dangers; but he is the true brave man, woman, or child, who dares to say "I have erred, forgive me."

II. Penal consequences of sin.

These divide themselves into two branches. 1. Those inflicted on the man. 2. Those inflicted on the woman.

1. Those inflicted on the man.

(1) The ground was cursed for his sake. "Thorns also and thistles shall it bring forth unto thee; in the sweat of thy face shalt thou eat bread" (ver. 18, 19). We must not suppose that for the first time then the law of labour entered into the world, but that then for the first time it was felt to be a curse; we must not suppose that thorns and weeds had no existence before the fall, but only that before that they had not seemed thorns and weeds to men. Every one knows that there is no weed grown in all God's earth that has not its appointed virtue, whilst science shows us daily that those once thrown aside as weeds are blessings to the world. The law of labour also is a curse only to those who will not submit to it; to others it is one of the best blessings of life. Adam's occupation before the fall was to dress the earth, and no doubt he found enjoy-

ment in his work ; and God's arrangement for us now is this :
for every mouth to be fed, for every body to be clothed, a pair
of hands ; for every intellectual work, a brain. Therefore it
comes to pass that if any man living in this world is doing nothing, he has taken away one pair of hands, one brain, from the
work of God, and left it to the performance of another.

(2) Death: "Dust thou art and unto dust shalt thou return."
Here again we must not think that if man had not sinned
his body would not have passed away, that death would not
have been. No ; but that death by sin became death ; otherwise it would have been simply a transition to a higher state of
being. What is it that makes the thought of death so horrible?
Is it not the weeping of friends around, is it not our own
want of faith ? All these things make it a thing to be feared.
Sin is the sting of death : take away sin, and you take away
with it death's terrors ; death becomes then as gentle as a
sleep. Stephen fell asleep. "The sting of death is sin, but
thanks be to God which giveth us the victory through our
Lord Jesus Christ." He hath blessed death.

2. Those inflicted on the woman.

"I will greatly multiply thy sorrow," etc. (ver. 16.) Compare this punishment pronounced on the woman with that on
the serpent as given in verses 14 and 15, and this apparently
startling difference is brought out. The penalty inflicted on
the weak seems terrible ; the penalty inflicted on the other is
merely this, that he shall go upon the dust, no pain at all
is imposed. Here is presented to us one of the mysteries of
Nature : the difference made between tempted frailty and
that selfish oppression which tempts frailty. The one suffers

terribly, is made an outcast from society, and endures the torments of a rebuking conscience; the other is often admired and seems free from all the stings of remorse. And upon all this the world looks with a strange indifference, and takes its stand with the oppressor. Let men say, and truly, that it is necessary to guard by the exaction of a penalty against the sin of frailty, we are bound also to retort the charge : if the consequences of frailty be terrible, it is the part of every brave man to avoid tempting frailty. If it be necessary to guard the keeper of the casket by penalties and pains, I ask what is the guilt and what the penalty belonging to the stealer of that casket? There is no ground whatever, no principle of justice, on which that infernal law of society can be defended which only punishes the feeble. When we turn to the life of Christ we find the voice of the Redeemer against it. He stands by the side of the weak and not of the strong. He shows no sympathy with those who have tempted frailty; He says : " Better that a millstone should be hanged about his neck, and that he should be cast into the sea, than that he should offend one of these little ones." And we know how He treated the frail, the publican and the sinner. On the one side then we have the voice of the Redeemer representing the voice of God, and that voice is on the side of frailty; but on the other hand we have the voice of Nature, also the word of God, and this voice appears to be against the frail : for it shows us frailty visited by terrible punishment whilst the oppressor goes free. How are we to reconcile this apparent contradiction? We turn to this third chapter of Genesis and we find our answer. God has two penalties for sin : one, the punishment of the offender, which is remedial, sharp, terrible, purifying ; another, the expression not of His paternal love but of His everlasting wrath ; no pain in that. Better for the punished if there were ! Look at this sin of Eve's. It was not a sin of sensuality. The temptation appealed not to her sensual but rather to her higher nature. The food was pleasant to the eye and to be desired to make one wise. Yet at the very instant she thought she was to be as God, knowing good and evil, she found herself, not as she had anticipated on the confines of heaven, but on the brink of hell. The chastisement which fell on her was terrible, but it was the remedial chastisement of love. It is that which frailty wants, and it is redeemed through it. Look at this penalty on the woman. what was its nature ? In sorrow she was to bring forth children, and her desire was to be to her husband, and he was to rule over her. This penalty of suffering for others, which is the very triumph of the cross, know we not its blessing ? Know we not that in proportion as we suffer for another we love that other ; that in proportion as the mother suffers for her child she is repaid by that love ? Know we not that that subjection which man calls curtailment of liberty is in fact a granting of liberty, of that gospel liberty which is born of obedience to a rule which men venerate and love ?

Indignation rises within the soul of every true man that one who has done unjust and oppressive wrong should go unreprehended ; that the daughters and wives of men calling themselves Christians are permitted to sit by such a man and to receive his patronage, when those to whom he has done the wrong are unheeded, cast out to perish. It is all just. The chain has bound itself around that man. Suffering will not hurt him; he will go on through this world happy. God has punished him, not with an ordinary punishment, but with the worst of punishments, a degradation worse than the agonies of hell itself, the punishment of being degraded and not knowing his own degradation. Would you give a man a penalty more terrible than this—to go upon the dust, to lead a degraded life day after day? If I speak to a man who has been perplexed by the moral government of the universe, to a man to whom this solution will give a burst of joy, because there is in it a vindication of the righteousness of God; to him I say the penalty is just which annexes suffering to frailty, and the serpent degradation to the reptile tempter.

LECTURE V.

Sunday Afternoon, June 2, 1850.

GENESIS xii.

THE eleventh chapter concludes that first great division of the Book of Genesis, in which we are given the history of the human race, a universal history; in the succeeding chapters the history ceases to be world wide, and becomes national. We do not and dare not say that God gave no revelation to any other nation except the Jews; all we know is this, that that given to the Jews is the only one of which we have any continuous record. Now the history of the Jews, at least the character of that history, is manifested in the character of the person from whom their national history begun. It is common to find that a nation imbibes the spirit of its founder. Nimrod, the founder of the Assyrian monarchy, was a conqueror, and the Assyrians were pre-eminently a conquering nation. But in the founder of the Jewish nation we find, not a conqueror, nor a lawgiver, but a saint, remarkable only for this, that he lived with God; and therefore we may expect to meet with what is really the case, not a profane history, but the history of piety.

The subject of this chapter divides itself into two branches :

I. The journey of Abram into the land of Canaan.

II. His journey into Egypt.

I. Abram's journey into the land of Canaan.

Observe here the gradual revelation and accomplishment of Abram's destiny. To understand this we must refer to the preceding chapter, where we learn (ver. 31) that Terah went up from Ur with his sons to go into Canaan, and when they came to Haran they dwelt there, and Terah died there. Abram was therefore now completing and fulfilling what Terah had begun; so that what at first seemed only a human plan is now clearly seen to be a Divine interference, for Abram's journey was made we are expressly told at the call of God. And this is the history of every one of us: gradually and slowly our destiny opens to us. Our Redeemer and Master teaches us not to be over anxious for the morrow, for we cannot discern its duties; all that belongs to us is to do the duty that lies before us to-day, and we may be sure of this, that when we have done the duty that is close before us we shall understand and see clearly the duties that lie beyond.

Observe again the number of the ties that were rent asunder when Abram left for Canaan. God told him to leave his country and his kindred and his father's house; till at last he was left in the world solitary. It matters not how this intimation was given to Abram; it is sufficient for us to know that it was given, and that he therein recognised the voice of God and immediately obeyed it. There is many a man called as Abram was, whose duty demands of him to quit the party with whom he has hitherto worked, to act again and again in such a way that those who have loved him will shrink from him; and, as it was with Abram and with Christ, he will find himself alone and solitary. There are many times when it must be so with us. We must learn to bear to live alone, not with regard to external things, but in our inward spirits.   Let us not be anxious to hear the hum of applauding voices round us, but be content to travel in silence the way which our Master travelled before.

Observe again the twofold nature of the promise given by God to Abram ; it was partly temporal, partly spiritual. The temporal promise was that he should have a numerous posterity, and that they should inherit Canaan ; and the spiritual promise was that he should be blessed (ver. 2).   Now this record was of great importance to Moses, who gave it to the people of Israel.   He was about to take Israel away from Egypt, and therefore he had to make them understand that the land they were going to was their own land, from which they were unlawfully kept out.   In proof of this he could refer to this promise of God to Abram.   Moses was revealing to the Israelites, surrounded by nations who worshipped many gods, the one true God.   He could tell them that it was no new God that he was thus teaching them to worship, but One who had appeared to their forefather Abram.

Observe once more the manner of Abram's journey through Canaan.   As he went along he erected altars to commemorate the mercies of God and to remind his posterity that this was really their own land.   Here we have that strange feeling of human nature, the utter impossibility of realizing the invisible except through the visible.   Churches, what are they built for ? To limit God and bind Him down to space ? or to explain God to us, to enable us to understand Him, and to teach us that not there *only* but in every place He is present ?   Consider then what the land of Canaan became.   Gradually it was dotted over with these stones, teaching the Israelites that it was a sacred land. What these stones did for the Israelites our memory does for us; it brings back in review our past life. Remember, I pray you, what that life will be to you when it all appears again. Blessed, thrice blessed, is the man to whom life is, as it was to Abram, dotted over with memorials of communion with God. But *your* life—that guilty thought and act, that unhallowed feeling—dare you see it come before you again? I pray you remember that this return of all the past to memory, in the day when God shall judge your life, is no dream, but one of the things that must be hereafter.

II. Abram's journey into Egypt.

At the court of Pharaoh Abram gained two of the most useful lessons of his life. He learnt that it is not in man that walketh to direct his steps; he became aware of his own weakness, and no doubt was cast henceforth in still more humble dependence upon God. And he learnt that all things work together for good to them that love God. We are ready enough to acknowledge that great things are in the hand of God; but we do not allow that the small circumstances of life, without which the journey to Egypt would not have been possible, are also under the guidance and direction of an all-wise God. But Abram found out this; for he came back from Egypt " very rich " in cattle, rich still more in a deepened faith in God and His law. The last was a spiritual possession strangely gained. It was gained in the midst of transgression; it is the glory of God to bring good out of evil. The transgression of Abram's was the saying that Sarah was his sister when she was his wife, and the saying was not distinctly false, but rather an evasion, for she was his half-sister. Now we do not say that every evasion is wrong. For example, when an impertinent question is asked respecting family circumstances or religious feelings it is not necessary that we should tell all. There are cases, therefore, in which we may tell the truth, though not the whole truth. It was even so with our Redeemer; for when asked by the Pharisees how He made Himself the Son of God, He would give them no answer. But it will be observed that Abram's evasion was nothing of this kind, it was a deception. It was not keeping back part of the truth when the questioner has no right to ask ; it was false expediency. It was a right expediency in Samuel when he permitted Israel to have a king, and the law of Christian expediency is to select the imperfect when the perfect cannot be had. It will be observed however that the expediency of Abram was altogether different. It was not the selection of the imperfect because the perfect could not be had, but it was the choice between telling the truth and saving his life; and Abram chose the falsehood that he might save his life—that is, he used an expediency which had nothing to do with Christian expediency. Of two blessings let the temporal blessing be the higher, and the spiritual blessing the lesser; still they are not commensurate. Man must not stop to ask himself which is best, right or wrong ; he *must* do right. It was on this principle that the blessed martyrs of old died for the truth ; it was but an evasion that was asked of them, but they felt that there was no comparison between the right and the wrong in the matter. "I have a life, you may take that : I have a soul, you cannot destroy that." It was thus they felt and acted.

There is but one apology that can be offered for Abram, and that is, the low standard of the age in which he lived; it must be remembered that he was not a Christian.

Lastly, we observe this, that Abram brought upon himself a rebuke from Pharaoh, the man of God was rebuked by the man of the world: a thing singularly humiliating. It is common to find men of the world whose honour and integrity is a shame to every Christian; and common enough to find men of religious feeling and aspiration, of whom that same world is compelled to say that whenever they are tried in business there is always a something found wanting. Salvation consists in this union of moral with spiritual character. Morality is not religion; but unless religion is grafted on morality, religion is worth nothing. Listen to the words of an apostle, " What doth it profit if a man say he hath faith and have not works, can faith save him?" Unless to faith is added virtue, we have not salvation.

LECTURE VI.

Sunday Afternoon, June 9, 1850.

GENESIS xiii.

WE have already entered into a class of subjects entirely different from that which has previously occupied our attention. We have been dwelling on the history of the world : we have now to consider the history of individuals. It follows that for some time to come our expositions will necessarily have more of a simple, humble, personal, practical character.

At the commencement of this chapter we have an account of the return of Abram from the land of Egypt, rich. It has been observed that the blessedness of the Old Testament is prosperity, while that of the New Testament is affliction. Let not men say from this that the law of God is altered ; it is we who have altered in conceptions of things. There was a time when men fancied that afflictions were proofs of God's anger, but the revelation of God in Christ has since manifested to us the blessedness of affliction ; for it is the cross that God bestows as His highest reward on all His chosen sons. But the chief subject of this chapter is the separation which took place between Abram and Lot. Let us observe the causes which rendered necessary this separation.

I. Prosperity. Poverty and trial made Abram and Lot cling closely to each other ; but the moment they reached prosperity a cause of separation arose between them. And this is the experience of life ; the enlargement of a man's possessions is very often the contracting of his heart. We learn from this the great doctrine of compensation; for almost every blessing must be paid a certain price. If a man would be the champion of the truth, he must give up the friendship of the world. Be sure of this, there is no rich and prosperous man we look at who has not paid his price––it may be in loss of domestic peace, in anxiety, or in enfeebled health; be assured that every earthly blessing is bought dearly.

II. The quarrelling among the servants; and this quarrel arose partly from disobligingness of disposition. Here we find the Christian community resembling the Jewish. There is a constant strife now among servants as to whose duty it is to do certain things, arising from the same indisposition to oblige one another. Then observe how by degrees Lot and Abram are drawn into the quarrel, and how again we find human nature the same in all ages. The bitterness between child and child, between husband and wife, are often to be referred back to the bitterness between domestic servants. Again, the scandal of this disagreement passed on through the land; the Canaanite and the Perizzite heard of it. Here is a lesson both for Christian masters and servants. Our very doors and walls are not sufficient to guard domestic secrecy; if there has been scandal in a place, that scandal is sure to be heard. And if Christian men and women listen to the gossip of their servants, I pray you with whom does the guilt lie? On the other hand, servants who wish to be servants not after the flesh but after the spirit, with good will doing service, as to the Lord and not unto men, should recollect that they are admitted into secrets which they must know, but that there is an honour which should bind their tongue. They are trusted ; they should let that trust be kept sacred for the Lord.

Now see how this separation between Abram and Lot, which might have resulted in a lifelong estrangement, was all put a stop to by Abram, first of all by his unselfishness. " Is not the whole land before thee? separate thyself I pray thee from me. If thou wilt take the left hand then I will go to the right ; or if thou depart to the right hand then I will go to the left " (ver. 9). This was noble, and it was an unselfishness that arose from his spiritual character, for he was not merely a generous man, but generous because religious. Secondly, his condescension stayed the quarrel. He was the elder, and therefore had the right to demand acknowledgment from Lot; but he waived his right. What a lesson for us: men often wish to make up a quarrel if the other would but come half way ; otherwise they think it would be against their honour to be reconciled. Brethren, a man's honour is not what men think of him. His honour consists in what he is. If in a quarrel one thing which should have been done has not been done, in the sight of God you are a dishonoured man. The third way in which Abram prevented this from becoming a settled quarrel was his wisdom in seeing that separation of place would prevent separation of heart. It is a lesson that we learn late in life. When once words of anger have been spoken we cannot recall them. It is wise to remember, when you are angry, that a quarrel may often be prevented by leaving the room when the unkind word is rising to the lip.

The chapter ends with a touching account of the Lord speaking to Abram. He had just lost his friend, and it was a moment in which you would have expected to find him left in bitterness; but instead of this the voice of God is heard telling him that the world is his. This is marvellously true to life. The promise was in the truest and most spiritual sense fulfilled here. Was it not fulfilled when he lifted up his spiritual eyes, and saw the garden of the Lord his Father's house, and if his Father's, might he not look upon it as his own too? Thus it is with us; when all is taken from us, then it is that we meet God more closely than before. God is not found in the crowd, but in silence, in solitude.

Lastly, contrasted with the unselfishness of Abram we see the selfishness of Lot. One would have fancied that an offer so generous as that of Abram would have transformed the heart of any man. But no! Lot does not seem to have been touched by it. He chose the rich land. It was nothing to him that the inhabitants were sinners before the Lord exceedingly; but in the end it mattered much. The result of his choice was the degradation of his family, the ruin of his happiness, so that he was left at last a bereaved old man. Yet this is just the way of the world now. Even religious men sometimes give themselves up as Lot to the love of the world; they will settle in a foreign country, notoriously licentious, merely that they may enjoy the scenery or live more economically; they will sacrifice their daughters for titles and wealth. But let every man and woman be assured of this, that God has terrible modes of retribution. In the choice of homes, of friends, and in alliances, he who selects according to the desires of the flesh and of the eye, and the pride of life—God has in store for that man retribution. If he will not be drawn by the cords of love, he must be driven by the rod of correction.

LECTURE VII.

Sunday Afternoon, July 28, 1850.

GENESIS xix.

THE nineteenth chapter of Genesis contains the conclusion of the dismal history of the cities of the plain. The guilt of Sodom and Gomorrah had been long ripe for judgment. They may be likened to a tree seared and blasted by the autumn winds, but having a few leaves on the topmost branches withered and dead; the next powerful gust of wind will dash them all to the earth. There are three subjects for our consideration in this chapter.

I. The destruction of Sodom and Gomorrah.

II. Lot's deliverance.

III. The fate of Lot's wife.

I. The destruction of Sodom and Gomorrah.

The doom of Sodom and Gomorrah was already fixed when God spoke with Abraham; but there had been delay, partly for Lot's sake, and partly for Divine reasons. The sun rose brightly that morning; but before it had sunk below the western horizon the blood was cold in many a breast that burned with unhallowed fire, and many a pulse had ceased to beat that a few hours before throbbed with selfish passion. Down came the burning red rain of fire from heaven, the fearful expression of the wrath of God. This strange flood of fire did for the bodies of men what death does for the soul. The attitude in which it found every man, there it sealed him. And so with death; it is the fixing of the form of the spirit in which each man dies, so to remain *for ever*. There is development, but no change in *all* the future. At the same time, when the cold hand of death changes the outward form, it but impresses on the spirit that form which is to remain for ever.

Let us now look at the agency which effected this destruction. The Bible refers it to the immediate action of God; and the truth of Scripture, it is thought by some, depends on establishing the miraculous character of the fall of these cities. A man goes now to the scene of the destruction of Sodom and Gomorrah, and tries to establish the fact that it was nothing but a natural volcanic eruption; and by getting rid of the super-natural agency he thinks he has got rid of God Himself. Another goes to the same place, and in his zeal for the super-natural wishes to make out that the veracity of the Bible depends on this kind of occurrence never having happened before. Do we mean then that only the *marvellous* incidents of nature,—the fall of a Sodom and Gomorrah taking place at an appointed time,—only the positive miracles, are God's doing, and not the commonplace events of every-day life? Nay, God holds all the powers of nature in His hand; small events *may* be so directed by Him that we shall think them accident; but for all this it is no less certain that the most trifling act of every-day life is directed by Him. What we have to say is this: we agree with the supernaturalist in saying that God did it; we agree with the rationalist in saying that it was done by natural means. The natural is the work of God.

Again, Scripture uses this destruction as the type of eternal punishment. It is written in Isaiah, "And Babylon, the glory of kingdoms, the beauty of the Chaldees' excellency, shall be as when God overthrew Sodom and Gomorrah." And again, St. Peter saith in his Second Epistle, "And turning the cities of Sodom and Gomorrha into ashes condemned them with an overthrow, making them an ensample unto those that after should live ungodly." And again, in the Epistle of St. Jude we read, "Even as Sodom and Gomorrha, and the cities about them in like manner, giving themselves over to fornication, and going after strange flesh, are set forth for an example, suffering the vengeance of eternal fire." So that throughout the Bible this destruction is used as the natural and symbolical expression of eternal punishment and God's judgment on the wicked. What this eternal punishment is, is described in the Revelation. There we read of the lake which burneth with fire and brimstone. Our education has gradually got rid of belief in the literalness of these words. Every one knows that they are symbolical; but with this it has unfortunately got rid of the deep truth which lies beneath these images. There is no lake which burneth with fire and brimstone; but there *is* the hell of doing wrong, the infinite maddening of remorse. When we remember what we *might* have been, and what we never can become, then we crave for a drop of water to cool our tongue, and there is no water to be found. *That* is the world of fire, *that* is the lake which burneth for ever. The law is written on our own hearts and the world around us. Sin, and you will suffer. As surely as the stone that is thrown up falls down to earth again, so surely does the penalty of an evil act come back, even after the lapse of centuries. Say you that, after a time, misery does its work? True, suffering *sometimes* does the work of repentance; but it oftener hardens the soul, and the sinner and sufferer sends back to Heaven the rebellious scream of defiance to his God. Sin *always* carries its penalty, but misery does not always lead to repentance.

II. Lot's deliverance.

Lot was a religious man, but a selfish man : selfish in the choice of the rich land to dwell in when he and Abraham separated; his prayer also was selfish, it was not like Abraham's prayer offered up for Sodom and Gomorrah. Lot only petitioned that God would save the city of Zoar, that he might there find a refuge. Here we perceive Lot's constant appeal to self interest, selfishness clung to that man's very soul. We should expect that after all the marvellous mercy shown by God to Lot, he would have been ready to go wherever He commanded. But no; Lot asks that Zoar may be saved. And God marvellously accepts this demand. Now this shows how God deals with the soul. We use large language; we talk of self sacrifice, self devotion, and yet there has always been the secret reservation of some small Zoar; still God accepts. He leaves us some human affection, something to remind us of our earthly home. He weans us by degrees, that so, step by step leaving earth behind, we may ascend the mountain top, and want nothing but the lovely love of God.

III. The fate of Lot's wife.

There was a great difference between the feelings of the

elder and the younger branches of Lot's family on leaving their home. His sons and daughters left it in apparent obedience, but with the spirit of the inhabitants of the plain; it was not so with Lot's wife. It is not the character of age to accommodate itself readily to fresh circumstances. The old man does not feel inclined to launch himself afresh on the great ocean of the universe, to seek new fortunes. He does not easily make fresh acquaintances or transplant himself quickly from old haunts and homes. To youth there is a future; to old age there remains nothing but the present and the past.

Therefore, while youth went on with its usual elastic step of buoyancy and hope, Lot's wife lingered; she regretted the home of her vanity and luxury, and the lava flood overwhelmed her, encrusted her with salt, and left her as a monument. The moral we are to draw from that is not left us to choose. Christ says, "Remember Lot's wife." It is worse to turn back, when once on the safe path, than never to have served God at all. They who have once tasted of the power of the world to come, let them beware lest they turn again. Sin is dangerous, but relapse is fatal. That is the reason why God so marvellously smooths the way for youth. Early joy enables the young man to make his first steps *surely*, with confidence in his Maker; love, gratitude, and all his best emotions are thus called forth. But if afterwards he falls, if he sinks back again into the world of evil, think you that his feelings will spur him on again in God's cause? Nay, because the first time there was hope, the next all the hope is washed out; the stimulus of feeling is weaker because experience has broken down hope; he knows now what those resolves were worth! There is a great difficulty in quitting evil after long habit. It becomes a home, and holiness is dull and cheerless and dreary. Youth then is the time for action—earnest, steady advancement, without looking back. St. Paul says, in his Epistle to the Hebrews, "Let us therefore fear lest, a promise being left us of entering into His rest, any of you should seem to come short of it;" and again he shows us the evil of drawing back, "Now the just shall live by faith: but if any man draw back, My soul shall have no pleasure in him." Our solemn watchword then should be, Forwards!

Finally learn from this chapter that God knows how to deliver the godly out of temptation. Abraham did not *fall* into temptation; temptation came upon him. It was not so with Lot; he surrounded himself with temptation. Twice the mercy of God rescued His strange infatuated servant. But the last time every tie was shattered, his home was in ruins, his wife dead, his children left him; and there Lot stood, at last, on the verge of the grave, an old broken-hearted sorrow-stricken man. Truly God knoweth how to deliver His people out of temptation, but it is often, as in Lot's case, an awful deliverance. And Abraham rose the next morning, full of anxiety, and turned his eyes towards Sodom and Gomorrah, now only one molten sea of fire. He contemplated the melancholy scene before him and felt with how fearful and solemn a gaze we should look on the miseries and punishments of those who do not fear God. It was then Abraham began secretly to understand the mystery of God's will and dealings with man; it was then the agonizing suspicion of God's justice, with which he had wrestled, found its solution. Lot was saved, the righteous were not destroyed with the wicked. The strange mystery of this hard, cruel, unintelligible world became plain; and the voice of his inmost heart told him, "All is right!"

This then explains those two magnificent contradictions, which, taken separately, are unintelligible, but which together form the basis of our faith: "God is love," but "our God is a consuming fire."

LECTURE VIII,

Sunday Afternoon, August 4, 1850.

GENESIS xxi.

WE omit the 20th chapter. The subterfuge was the same as that recorded in the 12th. The rebuke again came to the man of God from a child of this world. And this teaches us the difference between religious feeling and moral principle. It is one thing to have spiritual desires and aspirations; quite another to be true to them in practice. The chapter before us admits of two divisions.

I. The birth of Isaac.

II. The destinies of Ishmael.

I. Birth of Isaac.

Observe first the words of Sarah (ver. 6). "God hath made me to laugh, so that all that hear shall laugh with me." Evidently she is thinking of a former occasion when she greeted with the laugh of scepticism the prophecy which now had fulfilled itself. Quite different was Abram's laugh (chap. xvii. 5–17). It took place in a dream. It expressed his feeling of contentment. Let me be satisfied, it said, and not aspire to higher things than those given me.

Observe secondly the circumcision of Isaac. This was a sign of the covenant love of God towards the child, stamped upon him. Circumcision was an Egyptian not a Jewish rite. It was therefore an adopted ceremony, and a religious signification was now thrown into it. So it is with our rites of baptism, of the Lord's day, of the Supper of the Redeemer. These institutions were in existence before the time of Christ; He made them new by connecting them with new ideas. It is wise thus to vitalize existing forms, to infuse into them fresh meaning. We do not want new ones, the old are good enough for us; what we want is, to throw into the old a new life in order that that which is dying out may become alive. Circumcision was a coarse rite given to a coarse nation, a sign that they could understand; notwithstanding, they forgot that it was only a symbol. Prophet after prophet testified against this. As soon as the form began to lose its meaning and became substituted for the spiritual reality, it was proclaimed by our Master and His inspired servants that both were dead. And the fate of that institution is the fate of all form when it becomes nothing but *form ;* and men are wanted now who will say out with apostolic authority, baptism is nothing, the Lord's Supper is nothing, unless a living spirit be within them.

II. The destinies of Ishmael.

At the weaning of Isaac there was a feast. Hagar and her son heard the merriment, and it was gall to their wounded spirits; it looked like intentional insult; for Ishmael had been the heir presumptive, but now by the birth of Isaac had become a mere slave and dependant; and the son of Hagar mocked at the joy in which he could not partake. Wherefore Sarah said unto Abraham, "Cast out this bondwoman and her son" (ver. 10). These were harsh words : it was hard for one so young to have all blighted; it was grievous in Abraham's sight to witness the bitter fate of his eldest born.

And yet was it not the most blessed destiny that could happen to the boy? The hot blood of the Egyptian mother, which coursed through his veins, could not have been kept in check in the domestic circle among vassals and dependants; he was sent to measure himself with *men*, to cut out his own way in the world, to learn independence, resolution, energy; and it is for this reason that to this very day his descendants are so sharply stamped with all the individuality of their founder. In them are exhibited the characteristics of Abraham and Hagar, the marvellous devoutness of the one with the fierce passions of the other, and together with these the iron will, the dignified calmness of self dependence wrought out by circumstances in the character of Ishmael.

And how often is it that in this way the darkest day is the beginning of the brightest life. Reverses, difficulties, trials, are often amongst God's best blessings. From the loss of property is brought out very often the latent energies of character, a power to suffer and to act which in the querulous being without a wish ungratified you would have scarcely said had existed at all. The man compelled to labour gains energy, strength of character, the development of all that is within him. Can you call that *loss*? The richest resources are not from without, but from within. "Man's life consisteth not in the abundance of the things that he possesseth."

LECTURE IX.

Sunday Afternoon, August 11, 1850.

GENESIS xxii.

THIS chapter contains the history of the temptation of Abraham.

In the life of every one there has been one trial, one crisis, to which great issues are attached. Such was the trial we are to consider to-day, and therefore we call it *the* trial. Not that it was Abraham's *only* trial, but the chief one; for in truth all his life had been full of trials: trial, when he left his father's home to seek the land of Mesopotamia; trial in the land of Egypt, owing to the fears he entertained for Sarah's safety; trial when he parted with Lot; trial in the dreadful struggle of unbelief in God's dealings respecting the destiny of Sodom and Gomorrah; trial when, with the bitterness of a father's heart, he was forced to banish Hagar and her child; trial in his final separation from Ishmael; trial, and the worst trial of all, the black spot in his existence, when he remembered in his old age that he had no heir— a thought which corroded all his joy. Such was the inner history of one enjoying outward prosperity and peace, but whose inward life was full of struggles and suffering.

God tempted or tried Abraham. Christ was tempted in the wilderness. Life is all temptation. It is sad to think it so; but surely we would not have it otherwise. For dark and hard as the dispensation seems, trial here is indispensable for the purifying of the soul. There is no strength or real goodness of soul except that which is wrought out of circumstances of temptation; there is no strength in cloistered virtue, no vigour without trial. It is thus we can understand Abraham's life. In some of these trials he fell, and in others he came off victorious. He was by no means a perfect man, no specimen out of a romance. His was a *real* life. Out of failure was organized strength. Trials do not become lighter as we go on. The text says, "And it came to pass, *after these things*, that God did tempt Abraham." What, no repose? No place of honourable quiet for the "friend of God," full of years? No. There are harder and yet harder trials even to the end. The last trial of Abraham's was the hardest of all to bear. And this is the history of our existence. For the soldier engaged in *this* world's warfare, there is an honourable asylum for his declining years; but for the soldier of the cross there is no rest except the grave. Conquer, and fresh trials will be yours, followed by fresh victories. Nay, even Abraham's *last* victory did not guarantee the future. There is a deep truth contained in the fabled story of old, where a mother, wishing to render her son invulnerable, plunged him into the Styx, but forgot to dip in his heel by which she held him. We are baptized in the blood and fire of sorrow that temptation may make us invulnerable; but let us remember that trials will assail us in our most vulnerable part, be it the head, or heart, or heel. Let us therefore give up the idea of any moment of our lives coming when we may lay aside our armour and rest in perfect peace.

Our subject divides itself into three branches.

I. The difficulty and its explanation.

II. The nature of the trial.

III. The spirit in which it was sustained.

I. The difficulty and its explanation.

God seems to have required of Abraham what was *wrong*. He seems to have sanctioned human sacrifice. My reply is, God did *not* require it. You must take the history as a whole, the conclusion as well as the commencement. The sacrifice of Isaac was commanded at first, and forbidden at the end. Had it ended in Abraham's accomplishing the sacrifice, I know not what could have been said; it would have left on the page of Scripture a dark and painful blot. My reply to God's *seeming* to require human sacrifice is the conclusion of this chapter. God says, "Lay not thine hand upon the lad." This is the final decree. Thus human sacrifices were *distinctly* forbidden. He *really* required the surrender of the father's will. He *seemed* to demand the sacrifice of life.

But further still. God did not demand what was wrong. It did not *seem* wrong to Abraham. It is not enough defence to say God did not command wrong. Had God *seemed* to command wrong, the difficulty would be as great. Abraham's faith would then have consisted in doing wrong for the sake of God. Now it did not. Abraham lived in a country where human sacrifices were common; he lived in a day when a father's power over a son's life was absolute. He was familiar with the idea; and just as familiarity with *slavery* makes it seem less horrible, so familiarity with this as an established and conscientious mode of worshipping God removed from Abraham much of the horror *we* should feel. Let all this be borne in mind while we examine the history of Abraham's trial. For unless this was the case, Abraham did not show faith in obeying, but only a servile obedience to God's commands. For consider : if God's voice told Abraham to transgress the first rules of conscience, ought he not to have refused to obey God when He gave such a command? and ought he not to have reckoned it a horrible temptation of the devil? Faith would have been shown in disobeying the voice, and saying, This voice within me is God's, and *that* is not! Nay, it is of prime importance that we should remember that Abraham's moral conscience was *not* outraged by the command. There is no conflict more horrible than when two duties clash, as, for instance, in the case of Jephthah's vow, and of Herod's oath to the daughter of Herodias. It is more hideous still, if God's command, backed by a miracle, orders man to do that which His voice within forbids. I can see no escape then but insanity. Such *might* have been Abraham's case.

I dwell on this, because there is a possible delusion which it enables us to meet. To some men's minds, the idea presents itself of sacrificing conscience as a *duty*. They argue thus :— If it be noble to sacrifice *life* for God or man, how much more so is it to sacrifice your *soul ;* to tell a lie to save a life, to speak falsely in order to establish a doctrine, to sacrifice virtue for the sake of one loved, to surrender political principle to save one's party ! On this principle, men in ancient times performed pious frauds. This temptation to sacrifice conscience is often felt by those who are weakly good. Observe, had Abraham outraged his conscience, it would not have been faith, but sin ; and I say, reject such a thought as a Satanic temptation. He who sacrifices his sense of right, his conscience, for another, sacrifices the God within him ; he is not sacrificing self.

II. The nature of the trial.

We remark, first, this trial was made under aggravated circumstances. The words in which God's command was couched were those of accumulated keenness. God said, "Take now thy son, thine only son Isaac, whom thou lovest, and get thee into the land of Moriah," etc., etc. He with whom all thy future is connected—thy son, long expected and waited for, thine heir, full of promise and so dear to thee ! We can fancy, as the voice went on, that it seemed as if God took malignant pleasure in dwelling on every item of the suffering He was inflicting on Abraham. We can fancy Abraham crying in the bitterness of his soul, "Anything else but my only son. O Lord, not that !" Now the dreadfulness of all this was that Abraham had to think that God required this of him. He might have said, "My theology tells me God is love ; that He is my Father. I see no love in this demand. He seems to be nothing but an insatiate tyrant, demonstrating in this command the tyranny of His strength !"

My Christian brethren, forgive this blasphemy. I only put into words the rebellious feelings of many a heart if it had dared in the trial hour to say out all. Let any one remember the hour when he lost the friend he loved dearest and best on earth; and if he should recollect that he submitted to the trial with coldness and anger, he will be able to appreciate the manly resignation of Abraham. To subdue the father in the heart, *that* a Roman has done, and calmly signed his son's death-warrant; but to subdue it, not with Roman hardness, but with deep trust in God and faith in His providence, saying, It is not hate but love that requires this—this was the nobleness, this the fierce difficulty of Abraham's sacrifice; this it was which raised him above the Roman hero.

We remark, secondly, *Abraham* was to do this; his son was to die by his own hand, not by a delegate. It would have been a kind of relief to him, to have given the boy to the herdsmen that they might sacrifice him, that the father should not be asked to hear the dying shriek of the son. It would have been a relief, as in Moses' time, to have put the child into the river and trusted to circumstances to deliver it. But Abraham was not allowed to act as the Israelitish parents did in their semi-obedience to the kingly command, leaving matters to take their chance, hoping for some accident at last. He was to preclude escape. We do our sacrifices in a cowardly way; we leave loopholes for escape. We do not with our own hand, at His call, cut asunder the dearest ties. We do not immediately take the path of duty, but wait till we are forced into it; always delaying in the hope that some accident may occur which will make it impossible. Then conscience says, with a terrible voice: You *must* do it and with your *own hand*. The knife must be sharp and the blow true. Your own heart must be the sacrifice, and your own hand the priest. It must not be a sacrifice made for you by circumstances.

III. How the trial was met.

First. Without ostentation. Abraham rose early in the morning, and saddled his ass ; and when he arrived at the foot of Mount Moriah, he left the servants and went on with Isaac alone ; he wanted no witness to the deed.   Had the sacrifice taken place, he would have come back alone; there would have been none to blazon out the deed ; none to tell *how* it was done, how the father's lip trembled while the Hebrew's hand was firm.   It had to be done in secret, God alone seeing. There was no boast; no consciousness that he was doing a great and noble act; no analysis of feeling.   The men who make sacrifices are not those who talk about them.   Love of display, so common and so bad, is that which mars our sacrifices.   Those are true sacrifices which have been done alone and are hidden from the world.   The world knows too much of our feelings, and deeds, and sacrifices, and therefore the Redeemer demanded quietness, calmness, and secrecy with respect to our alms, prayers, and sacrifices.

Secondly.   Abraham was in *earnest*.

We remark two things particularly : Abraham did not tell Sarah.   Had he told her, the mother's heart would have pleaded, her love would have marred the act, her shrieks would have roused her neighbours, and the deed would not have been done.   Do we not know how when a painful deed has to be done a man tells some weaker being,—his sister, or his mother, or his wife,—hoping secretly that they will dissuade him from his purpose, and prevent the doing of that which it would be a shame for him to prevent.   They will hinder him, or perhaps with entreaties and tears excuse him to himself.   It was not so with Abraham.   He did not tell Sarah ; he did not tell

Isaac; he kept the matter secret in his own bosom, simply because he was in earnest. Abraham *meant* his son's life. There
are many who were once perchance just on the brink of a noble
deed, and they take credit to themselves that had no circumstances intervened the deed would have been done. Remember,
their deed was *not* done. Are we sure they ever really *meant* to
do it? In Abraham there was really the belief that he would
come back childless. Had he expected what took place, it had
been no sacrifice. Some persons make sacrifices, expecting to
be repaid. They say and teach: Do right, and you will not
be the worse; give up, and somehow or other God will make
it up to you. True, " he that giveth to the poor lendeth to the
Lord." But if you do it with that feeling, your reward is lost; it is
not religion but mere traffic, barter; you only sacrifice little, in
order to gain much. If you make a sacrifice, expecting that God
will return you your Isaac, that is a sham sacrifice, not a real
one. Therefore, if you make sacrifices, let them be *real*. You
will have infinite gain: yes; but it must be done with an earnest
heart, expecting nothing in return. There are times too when
what you give to God will *never* be repaid in kind. Isaac is
not always restored; but it will be repaid by love, truth, and
kindness. God will take you at your word: He says, " Do
good and lend, hoping for nothing in return."

Let us consider three things, in conclusion.

First, the Christian sacrifice is the surrender of will.

God did not require Abraham to shed his son's blood; but
He required the surrender of his will. He demands the entire
surrender of ourselves to His Divine will; and when that is
freely, unhesitatingly given, then He saith, " Now I know that

thou fearest God, seeing thou hast not withheld thy son, thine only son, from Me." This explains to us the great principle of the atonement. The death of Christ was the world's Atonement; He made the great sacrifice for us all. This was acceptable to God, not because He delights in the shedding of blood; but because He demands the surrender of *will*, the blending as it were of the human with the Divine. "Lo, I come; in the volume of the book it is written of Me, to do Thy *will*, O God!" The surrender of will is the Christian's sacrifice.

Secondly, for a true sacrifice, there must be real love.

God says, "thy son *whom thou lovest.*" Some people would have been inclined to say, Abraham did not love his son; or he could not have sacrificed him! But I say, had Abraham not been willing to part with Isaac into the hands of God, his love even to Isaac would have been feeble. He who prefers his dearest friend or his well-beloved child to the call of duty will soon show that he prefers himself to his dearest friend, and would not sacrifice himself for his child. A man does not really love his friend who does not love his honour more.

Third, we must not *seek* for sacrifices.

We often say, What shall I do for God? Every earnest mind wishes to sacrifice to God. Be not anxious; you need make no wild, romantic efforts to find occasions. Plenty will occur by God's appointment, and better than if devised by you. Every hour and moment our will may yield as Abraham's did, quietly, manfully, unseen by all but God. These are the sacrifices which God approves. This is what Abraham meant when he said "My son, God will provide Himself a lamb for a burnt offering."

LECTURE X.

Sunday Afternoon, October 20, 1850.

GENESIS xxiii.

WE now find ourselves in the midst of the history of Abraham, and to-day our attention must be drawn to him beside his wife's grave. From this dates the first fact that hallowed the land of Israel. There is something touching in this; the land became holy first by a grave. And this teaches us that life is to be looked upon more properly as a grave than as a home, for in it are buried all our hopes and promises, to rise again in after life purified and ennobled. The chapter before us admits of two divisions.

I. The circumstances that attended the death of Sarah.

II. Those connected with her burial.

I. The circumstances that attended the death of Sarah.

The first thing which strikes us in connection with the death of Sarah is the rapid succession of events. Only a few chapters back we were reading of Sarah's marriage, and the birth of her child : now we are told of her funeral. Of course there is some illusion here. From the comprehensive character of the Bible biographies related in short chapters, much must necessarily be omitted ; we get results rather than the train of circumstances that led to them. Yet really this represents life. Life is but a few chapters. We stand by the font, are surprised when we find ourselves by the altar, astonished when we come to die. Death is *the* solemn thought of the world. Let it be ever so vulgarized or common; still, beneath the tent of the eastern emir or in the crowded cemeteries of the capital, death is an awful arresting thing. While civilization has robbed other horrors of their wonder death is still the insoluble event. But here we have something more than death, we have separation. Abraham and Sarah had lived together for long, but they were parted at last. The shock was broken in Abraham's case by its naturalness. The dissolution of the aged is expected; and often the survivor dies soon.

Two results this separation had upon Abraham. First: it realized and forced upon him the thought of his own mortality, for we find him saying to the children of Heth that he is a stranger and sojourner in the land. Thus it is with us. Death becomes awfully credible when those we are accustomed to live with die. We feel then as those tell us they have felt who have experienced an earthquake. The earth, the most stable of things, becomes to them unstable, and to us the solid life becomes hollow, and " I may be the next" is the first thought. Death comes home to us when we are the next to go.

Next, this separation had another result on Abraham. It made him realize his immortality. What is our evidence of a future life? It is our affections. Surely not that life must *per se* continue. Our bodies perish: mind may perish as well. It is not life, mere life, that must last. It is not more difficult to conceive life ceasing than life beginning. Once we were not, soon we shall not be. Why not? It is by our infinite affections reaching out after the infinite, that we feel that there must be a future. The immortal part of us, severed, bleeding, seeks when one we love is dead with its quivering feelers for the lost part. We are Sadducees till we lose one we really and deeply love; then, when our hearts are widowed, we strain our eyes and see beyond. So we may think that Abraham's grief ("and Abraham came to mourn for Sarah and weep for her," ver. 2) enabled him to pierce the veil that separates this life from the next. And this leads to another circumstance attending Sarah's death, Abraham's tears. Observe here the beautiful simplicity of Scripture, which counts it not a thing unmanly to own that Abraham, the stern, iron hearted saint, had wept. "Joseph lifted up his voice and wept"; Jacob, Peter, Christ, are all said to have wept. Contrast this with the conventional feeling which represents grief as unworthy of manhood, chokes tears as feminine, or rebukes them as inconsistent with submission to the will of God.

Again, in those tears of Abraham was anguish; but there might have been remorse. Apparently Abraham had nothing to reproach himself with. Quarrels in his married life are recorded; but in all he behaved with tenderness, concession, and dignity. In all things he had supported and cherished his wife, bearing, like a strong man, the burdens of the weak. But oh, let *us* beware. There are bitter recollections which enhance the sorrow of bereavement and change it into agony, recollections which are repeated to us in words which remorse will not cease to echo for ever and for ever. "Oh, if they would but come again, I'd never grieve them more." It is this which makes tears scald; to how many a grown heart have not those childish words of the infant hymn gone home, sharp with an undying pang !

II. The circumstances connected with Sarah's burial.

Observe in the first place the honour which the ancients paid to the dead. What does this prove? It proves that they too had a secret glimmer of immortality. Children cannot believe the dead extinct ; they talk of them as scarcely gone. So it was in the childhood of the world. The Egyptians anticipated reanimation. Simple early nations always seem to have felt the dead living still.

Observe again, under this division, the transaction with the children of Heth. It is often supposed to have been an instance of extraordinary liberality on their part; but it was not so. It was an eastern custom, as all travellers know, that of exchanging gifts ; but they were gifts which entailed an obligation. The receiver found himself pledged to give at least as large an amount as he had received. Here therefore in the words of Ephron to Abraham, " Nay, my lord, the field give I thee, and the cave that is therein I give it thee" (ver. 11), we have simply a conventional mode of speech. Abraham asks for a burying place. It is offered as a gift. Abraham understands what is meant, refuses, and pays for the ground. Ephron after a show of reluctance consents to receive payment; but all was well understood and common.

Here is a scriptural precedent for exactitude in business Notice the strict attention which Abraham paid to having the contract drawn up in due form ; for the 17th and 18th verses of this chapter are evidently an extract from some legal document. They read like a deed of conveyance

F

The boundaries of the field are accurately defined, and all the perquisites going along with it—the trees, and cave. Abraham acts throughout as a man of business; it was not pride on his part, but justice and prudence. He could afford to pay, and why should he receive? From a friend, well; but from a stranger it was neither just nor prudent. And this exactitude was of more religious import-ance than at first sight appears. It was a means of preventing future misunderstandings. Quarrels arise often from false delicacy. It is painful to speak of terms, to introduce into questions especially so delicate as this bartering and bargain-ing about money. One party in an agreement knows he means generously, and trusts the other. But each forms a different estimate of rights; one exaggerates, the other depreciates, the service done. It is from such undefined boundaries and limitations, from non-distinctness between the mine and the thine, from the use of such phrases as "what you please," that quarrels and dissensions most frequently occur. There-fore Abraham reads a lesson to men of business, and to those whose habits are not those of business. Doubtless there is a Christian way of bearing the consequences of neglect—it is, not to dispute at all; but it is better, if possible, to arrange so that no cause for dispute should arise; and Abraham says as it were to each of us, Let every agreement be distinctly and accurately made, for the sake, not of interest, but peace and charity.

Observe also how courteous phrases contain a higher ex-cellence than they mean. "What is that betwixt me and thee?" The children of Heth had no intention whatever of being taken at their word, any more than a man has now when he calls himself your humble servant or bids you command him. We must go back to an earlier age when phrases were coined and meant something, when gifts were gifts and nothing was hoped for in return, in order to catch the life that was once in our conventional phraseology. So now language preserves, as marble preserves shells of hoar antiquity, the petrified phrases of a charity and humbleness which once were living. They are dead, but they do at least this, they keep up memorials of what should be. So that the world, in its daily language of politeness, has a record of its duty.

Take those phrases, redeem them from death, live the life that was once in them. Let every man be as humble, as faithful, as obedient as his language professes, and the kingdom of God has come !

Lastly, we find in connection with Sarah's burial a Divine provision for the healing of Abraham's sorrow. He was compelled to exert himself to obtain a place to " bury his dead out of his sight." Had he not had to rouse himself and procure a grave for Sarah, he would have brooded over his grief. This is the merciful plan of compensation which God has provided for us; the necessities of life call us from our sorrow. All these merciful provisions plainly show us that we are in a Father's world.

LECTURE XI.

Sunday Afternoon, October 27, 1850.

GENESIS xxiv.

WE come to-day to the subject of marriage. There are two aspects in which it may be viewed—as a natural institution, and as a religious ordinance. In the Old Testament we see it as a natural institution; in the New it is brought before us in a religious light, for we are there shown its spiritual significance, it is there likened to Christ and the church. Now, what is remarkable here is, that the union of Christ and the church is not illustrated by marriage, but marriage by this spiritual union, that is, the natural is based upon the spiritual. And this is what is wanted; it gives marriage a religious signification and it thus becomes a kind of semi-sacrament. Now there are two points in which this illustration holds good: first, in the nature of the union, for in marriage, as in the union between Christ and His church, like is joined to unlike. The other point of resemblance is in the principle of sacrifice, for as no love between man and wife can be true which does not issue in a sacrifice of each for the other, so Christ gave Himself for His church and the church sacrifices itself to His service. The only true love is self devotion. Thus we see how all, even the every day affairs of married life, must fail without this principle of the cross of Christ. In the subject of this chapter there are three things that we must notice.

I. The embassy of Abraham's servant.

II. The discharge of that mission.

III. The arrival of Rebekah at her husband's home.

I. The embassy of Abraham's servant.

Here observe, in the first place, that this delicate mission was delegated to a servant or slave, because Isaac, according to the notions of those days, was too inexperienced to go himself. The choice, however, was not left to the servant, it was rather left to God. Abraham said to the servant : " The Lord before whom I walk will send His angel with thee and prosper thy way" (ver. 40). We next observe the touching confidence which subsisted between master and servant. And in this we learn (ver. 40) in what true liberty consists : this man was a servant,—a slave if you will ; and yet he enjoyed far greater liberty than our modern servants, who are free to go where they please; his freedom consisted in that glorious principle of obedience through love which makes a man free at once and which we have so grievously forgotten. The third thing that we notice in this embassy is that the servant was enjoined by oath to undertake his master's commands. This was allowable in Judaism ; but Christ says, "Swear not at all." Our nay is to be nay and nothing else but nay, and our yea yea ; the word of the Christian is to be so true that no oath could add to its security. But what Abraham meant to express was this, that he would hold the man firm to his word by religious fear and duty. There are two ways of speaking truth : many a man may be true from expediency, and this may last so long as he sees he shall gain by being true ; but as soon as an opportunity appears for winning something by falsehood without any immediate evil consequences, then his truth is at an end. Truth, to be constant, must lean upon a religious basis.

II. The discharge of the mission : observe here the servant's expectation of Divine help. He at once knelt down and asked for guidance (ver. 12, 13, 14). What a lesson may we not gain from that ! If, however, we were *exactly* to imitate this act of Abraham's servant, we should be wrong, though it was right in him. For he prayed that the woman he was to choose might appear to him at the well. This would be wrong in us, for this reason, that Jesus condemned the use of signs ; with us it would be an appeal to chance, but in the case of the servant it was done in faith. We next observe the principle on which the selection was made ; the qualities required were amiability, sincerity, and modesty. In this we see the inspired judgment with regard to woman's character ; it was formed of qualities of the heart rather than of the intellect ; qualities belonging less to the duties of public than to those of domestic life ; for God has given to women to shine, not so much in brilliancy of mind as in warmth of affection.

III. Rebekah's arrival. She found Isaac engaged in prayer and meditation ; two things from which we have sadly fallen. We are not the giants in prayer that our fathers were. We read here that as soon as Rebekah knew that her husband was coming she alighted from her camel, and took a veil, and covered herself. And this, brethren, is what we so much want ; I know it to be the bane of domestic life, the want of modesty and delicacy ; without Rebekah's veil affection becomes alienated, and often turns to hatred ; love, to be constant, must be kept pure.

LECTURE XII.

Sunday Afternoon, November 3, 1850.

GENESIS XXV.

AT the close of the last chapter Abraham was in years;
Isaac in the prime of life, and lately married to Rebekah.
At the close of this Abraham is gone, Isaac stricken in years,
and the offspring of his marriage grown men. And such is life;
one generation passing off the stage, another coming on. As
the sun passing over the world gilds mountain top after mountain top, valley after valley, then leaves all in gloom; so each
man has his hour and day of work, then "the night cometh,
when no man can work." The chapter for to-day is divided into
two branches. The first, from verses 1 to 18, gives an account
of a generation whose history is retrospective; that history is
represented by the closing years of Abraham's life. The
second division, from verses 18 to 34, treats of a generation
whose history is prospective; that history is represented by
the birth of Esau and Jacob.

I. History that is retrospective.

Our first remark here is the arising of new hopes in the
declining years of Abraham. Sarah is dead; and when
Abraham bowed himself before the sons of Heth his heart
seemed buried in Sarah's grave. Isaac was married, and all
Abraham's care seemed to centre in him. Yet here we find
Abraham contracting a new alliance, busied about life, entering

with energy into a fresh sphere of duties. We collect from that the imperishable nature of hope. No *natural* sorrow is eternal. When Paul and Barnabas parted, one would have thought that their hearts so violently torn asunder would have been long ere they had healed, but soon we find each twining round a new friend with as much warmth of affection as before. Out of the grave fresh hopes bloom; for our affections are not meant to rest in their objects, but to pass on from one thing to another. They are prospective. They exist here in training for nobler uses. They are perennial, and unless exhausted by misuse grow ever fresher and stronger to rest on God at last. We also notice that Abraham established the right of primogeniture. He gives all that he has to Isaac, gifts only to the rest. Two nations only among the ancients kept up the notions of family, the Romans and the Jews. In all other nations a man rested on his own title to consideration, on his own merits. In these two a man gathered family associations and national ones as his race went on. The Jews said, we are Abraham's seed, descendants of Abraham, Isaac, and Jacob, and there was an advantage in their feeling children of this long ancestry, because those who have a great past get out of self. They are pledged not to dishonour their ancestors. Many, by the mere stirring of such a memory, are dignified. They who have no past have a certain vulgarity, or uneasiness; or else personal pride differs from the dignity which knows whence it comes.

And this, in a way, is the Christian's advantage. We have a past. We stand upon a past; it is a righteousness not our own which has shed its lustre on us. We do not make our own destiny or heaven. These are gifts given us, advantages and privileges, but we have no merit in possessing them. Hence the Christian's sense of dignity is humble, for it is not personal but derived.

It may be that the privilege of having a past genders pride in us. There is a corrective to that given us in this chapter, for we are told here that the elder shall serve the younger. The whole Bible contradicts the extravagant pretensions of hereditary birth. Consider Cain and Abel; David and Eliab; Ishmael and Isaac; Esau and Jacob; Reuben and Judah. The whole Jewish system, built on the system of family, was yet contradicted at every stage; for was not Cain's offering rejected, while that of the younger, Abel, was accepted? Again, was not Isaac set before Ishmael? The children of Abraham are the spiritual seed; noble, if noble in character; but if untrue to the past only to be counted the more ignoble. We are great in being Englishmen; but unless children in spirit of those who have shed lustre on the English name, our advantages are our shame.

And so it is with us as members of the church, and as Christians.

Again we notice Abraham's experience. He stood now an old man on the brink of the grave. Let us hastily recapitulate his history, so chequered by vicissitudes. He began his wanderings at Charran; then seeking a new country, he entered Canaan, feeding his flocks there as long as pasture lasted, and then passed on. After that we find him still a wanderer, driven by famine to Egypt; then returning home, parting with Lot, losing his best friend, commanded to give up the dearest object of his heart, and at last at the close of life startled almost to find that he had not a foot of earth in which to make for his wife a grave. Thus throughout his life he was a pilgrim. In all we see God's blessed principle of illusion by which He draws us on towards Himself. The object of our hopes seems just before us, but we go on without attaining it; all appears failure, yet all this time we are advancing surely on our journey and find our hopes realized not here but in the kingdom beyond. Abraham learnt thus the infinite nature of duty, and this is what a Christian must always feel. He must never think that he can do all he ought to do. It is possible for the child to do each day all that is required of him; but the more we receive of the spirit of Christ, the larger, the more infinitely impossible of fulfilment will our circle of duties become.

We also observe this in Abraham, that he was not a hero but a saint. There have been three ages of the world. 1. That in which power was admired, when strength, personal prowess, was the highest virtue; then God was described as "a man of war." 2. That in which wisdom was reverenced. Then we have Solomon the wise, instead of Saul the strong; and then the wisdom of God is felt to be in contrivance, rather than in power. 3. That in which goodness was counted best. Then God and nature were felt to be on the side of right, and virtue was counted better than wisdom; that is the age in which Christianity can begin, the fulness of times is come. And it is three such seasons that we personally go through. In boyhood we reverence strength. In youth, intellect. In riper years, the milder graces of the heart. Now what is remarkable is, that Israel began with, not a hero, nor a wise man, but a saint. Abraham is not the warrior, nor the sage, but the father of the faithful. Hence the perennial, progressive character of the Jewish religion. It is not a thing that can come to an end. Abraham, the man of faith, is the forerunner of the Lord of Love.

II. The history that is prospective, represented by the birth of Esau and Jacob. Observe here how again the Jewish race is divided.

All the previous history has been a division into two lines. First, the line of Abraham divides into that of Israel and Ishmael : Israel is chosen, Ishmael rejected. Then the line of Israel subdivides into those of Esau and Jacob : Jacob is chosen, and Esau rejected.

And such has been God's way. Of the Jews carried away captive into Babylon only a remnant returned. All those belonging to the visible church are not members of the true invisible church. There will be at the end of the world, we are told, one taken and the other left. Many are called but few chosen, a chosen few like the three hundred separated from Gideon's army. Of these two boys, Esau and Jacob, we see in one the gross man of the world, in the other a character far higher, though mixed with a certain craft or cunning. This sin was not repressed in youth, and it grew up with him into manhood. It is always so : unless the evil propensity is checked in childhood it will increase as life goes on, and that most wise saying is verified, " the child is father of the man." Esau is called in the Epistle to the Hebrews a profane, that is a worldly person. His life was one of impulse, wanting in reverence, without any sensitive appreciation of things not level to his senses. Imprudent, incontinent, unable to restrain himself, he sacrificed the future to the present; he looked not beyond the passing hour; he sold his soul for pottage. We can scarcely account for his being the best beloved of his father, except on the principle of like joining to unlike.

LECTURE XIII.

Sunday Afternoon, November 17, 1850.

GENESIS xxvi.

THE chapters which have come before us in our exposition have generally afforded us one connected subject, but it is not so with this chapter. It contains many unconnected circumstances, and therefore our exposition this afternoon must necessarily be of a somewhat desultory character. There are three points upon which we shall have to touch : first, the famine ; secondly, the falsehood of Isaac ; and thirdly, Isaac's prosperity.

I. The famine.

Here the first thing that suggests itself is the apparent contradiction of the promise given to Abraham, for instead of the land of abundance and rest Isaac found famine and unrest. Let us endeavour to understand that, and then we shall better understand this life of ours ; for our life is to us a Canaan, a land of abundant promises, and especially so in youth. But we have not been long in this land of promise before we begin to discover that it falsifies itself, and then there arises in our mind the question that must have presented itself to Isaac, Has God broken His promise? We say God's promise, because the promises of life are all permitted by Him. The expectation of happiness is God's creation ; the things which minister to happiness are scattered through the world by God.

But if we look deeper into it we shall perceive that God does not deceive us. True it is, that Isaac was disappointed; he got no bread, but he did get perseverance. He did want comforts, but with this want came content, the habit of soul-communion with God. Which was best, bread or faith? Which was best, to have abundance, or to have God? Tell us then: had God broken His promise? Was He not giving a double blessing, far more than He promised? And so it is with us. Every famine of the soul has its corresponding blessing; for, in truth, our blessed hours are not those which seem so at first; and the hours of disappointment, which we are tempted to look upon as dark, are the ones in which we learn to possess our souls. If, in the worst trial earth has, there does not grow out of it an honour which could not else have been, a strength, a sanctity, an elevation; if we do not get new strength, or old strength restored, the fault is ours not God's. In truth the blessed spots of earth are not those which at first sight seem so. The land of olive and vine is often the land of sensuality and indolence. Wealth accumulates and engenders sloth and the evils which follow in the train of luxury. The land of clouds and fogs and unkindly soil, which will not yield its fruit unless to hard toil, is the land of perseverance, manhood, domestic virtue, and stately and pure manners. Want of food and of the necessaries of life, I had well-nigh said that these things are not an ill, when I see what they teach; I had well-nigh said I do not pity the poor man. There are evils worse than famine. What is the real misfortune of life? Sin, or want of food? Sickness, or selfishness? And when I see Isaac gaining from his want of food the heart to bear up and bear right onward, I can understand that the land of famine may be the land of promise, and just because it is the land of famine.

We observe in the second place, respecting this famine, that the command here given to Isaac differed from that given to Abraham and Jacob. Isaac evidently wished to go down to Egypt; but God forbad him (ver. 2, "Go not down into Egypt"), although He permitted Abraham and commanded Jacob to go thither. The reason for this variety is to be found in the different characters and circumstances of these men. In the New Testament we find the same adaptation of command to character. The man of warm feelings who came to Jesus was told that "the foxes have holes, and the birds of the air have nests : but the Son of Man hath not where to lay His head." When the man from whom the legion of devils was cast out besought Jesus that he might be with Him, he received a similar rebuff; but the man of lukewarmness, who wanted to return to bury his father and mother, was not permitted for an instant to go back. The reason of the difference is this, that the man of impetuosity and forwardness needed to be restrained, while the lingering and slow man needed some active measure to stir him forward. It is almost certain that Abraham, being a wise man and a man of faith, was permitted by God to judge for himself, and that Isaac was required to turn back that he might learn the duty of trust, and that Jacob was commanded to go forth in order to cure his love of the world and to teach him that life is but a pilgrimage. Hence we arrive at a doctrine : duties vary according to differences of character. The young rich man had a call to give up all ;

that is not every man's duty. One man may safely remain in a place of idleness and luxury, having a martyr's spirit; whereas to another his own temperament, soft and yielding, says as with God's voice, Arise for thy life, look not behind thee, escape to the mountains. Hence too we learn another lesson: the place in which we are is generally God's appointed place for us to work in. Isaac was prohibited from going forth. He was commanded not to wait for another set of circumstances, but to use those he had, not in some distant moment, but here, now, in the place of difficulty. And you: *do not wait* then for a more favourable set of circumstances; take them as they are, and make the best of them. Those who have done great things were not men who have repined that they were not born in another place or age, but those who did their work from day to day. It is not in moving from place to place that we find rest, in going down into Egypt because present circumstances seem unfavourable. No. Here where we are placed, even in the land of famine, in the dearth and darkness, we are to toil.

II. Isaac's falsehood: ver. 7.

The history of Uriah and David makes it easy to understand how such falsehoods came to be spoken; for in those un-scrupulous days a stranger ran a risk of being put to death on some pretext that a royal tyrant might take his wife in mar-riage. We find that Abraham committed this very sin of lying twice before. Now in Isaac's case this certainly would account for, though by no means excuse, his lie. He had before him the example of his father's cowardly falsehood. And he copied it. We are thus ever prone to imitate the characters of those we admire. Their very failings seem virtues; and hence comes a solemn consideration, that a good man's faults are doubly dangerous; the whole weight of his authority is thrown into the scale; his very virtues fight against God. Another thing which will help to explain Isaac's act is an idiosyncrasy of character. He was possessed of a kind of subtilty, an over fine edge of mind; and the tendency of this is toward craft and cunning. Such characters see both sides of a question; go on refining and refining, weighing points of subtil casuistry, until at last they become bewildered and can scarcely see the border line between right and wrong. It requires characters like Abimelech's, rude, straightforward, to cut asunder the knot of their difficulties.

Observe again how this tendency to falsehood through over refinement is seen in Jacob also, Isaac's son : thus it is that characters are handed down from father to son.

Remark too another quality which accompanies such characters as Isaac's, want of courage : " lest I die for her." Contemplative men, who meditate at eventide, who are not men of action, want those practical habits which are oftentimes the basis of truthfulness.

It is a want especially remarkable now. Never was there a day in which this tone of mind was more common or more dangerous. Our day is not remarkable for devoutness ; and the men who are so are not remarkable for manliness. They have somewhat of effeminacy in their characters, are tender, soft, wanting a firm, broad footing on reality. It is just to such minds as these that the Church of Rome offers peculiar attractions. She appeals to all that craves for awe, reverence, tenderness, mystery. Men get to live in mystery

and shadows, and call it devoutness. Then in this border-
land, between reality and unreality,—this cloud region as it
were,—truth itself melts away by degrees. Is it not an
indisputable fact that, so soon as men leave our Church for
Rome, their word is not to be trusted; that they get a
double dealing spirit, a habit of casuistry, and of tampering
with truth on plausible and subtle pretences which is a dis-
grace to Englishmen, not to say Christians? Therefore, let
religious life strengthen itself by action. We want a more
real life. A life merely prayerful, spent in dim religious
lights, amidst the artistic parts of religion, architecture,
chantings, litanies, fades into the unreal and imaginary.
And the unreal and merely imaginative soul passes into the
false soul.

III. Isaac's prosperity: ver. 12, 13, 14. "And Isaac sowed
in that land and received in the same year, an hundredfold
and the Lord blessed him. And the man waxed great and
went forward, and grew until he became very great, for he
had possession of flocks and possession of herds, and great
store of servants. And the Philistines envied him." Observe
Isaac's prosperity was not unalloyed. He suffered from envy.
Be sure of this, that for every blessing man pays a price.
If the world has gained in medical skill, it has lost that
simple life which made it unnecessary. If we heap possessions round us, we lose quiet, we get anxiety. Every man
pays a price for his advantages, for talents, for property, for
high station; he bids adieu to rest, being public property.

It was so with Isaac. He had great possessions, "and the
Philistines envied him." We are told that he met the envy

with patience, and removed from well to well. At last the Philistines desisted. Thus patience wears the world out. Endurance, meekness, the gospel spirit, this is the only true weapon against the world. Hence, Christianity can have no addition. It is final. There is nothing beyond this—"Love your enemies." Isaac like Christ had conquered by meekness; and then it was that there was shed abroad in his heart that deep peace which is most profound in the midst of storm, "the peace of God which passeth all understanding." God was with him (ver. 24): "And the Lord appeared unto him the same night, and said, I am the God of Abraham thy father : fear not, for I am with thee and will bless thee and multiply thy seed for My servant Abraham's sake." The waves which lash the surface of the sea are only on the surface ; below, the deeps are calm. And Isaac quietly leaving place after place felt the deeps of his soul untouched. What was the loss of a well, or ten wells, to him with whom God was, for his portion, his exceeding and all-sufficient great reward ?

Again mark another instance of this forgiving spirit of Isaac in his conduct to Abimelech. A wrong had been done him, and he forgave it on Abimelech's entreaty. Observe, however, it was no weak forgiveness. There are men who forgive everything, because they cannot feel strongly, like Cranmer ; gentle without sense of wrong ; only apathetic. Isaac was different by temper. He keenly felt the wrong, could resent it, and be indignant. When Abimelech came to him with his friends he answered them, "Wherefore come ye to me, seeing ye hate me, and have sent me away from you?" (ver. 27.) It was not feeling, but principle, that made him forgive. So too Christ's was no feeble voice. He could be indignant, and yet pity and forgive. He had a keen sense of injustice: "Why smitest thou Me?" Yet His last word was, "Father, forgive them, for they know not what they do."

This reconciliation between Isaac and Abimelech was pledged in a feast. They both sware unto one another: so is our reconciliation with God pledged in the Christian feast of the Lord's Supper.

LECTURE XIV.

Sunday Afternoon, December 1, 1850.

GENESIS xxvii.

IN chapter xxv. we find Abraham preparing for death by a last will, making Isaac his heir and dividing the remainder of his property in legacies among the children of Keturah. In this chapter the heir himself is preparing to die. The rapidity with which these chapters epitomize life, bringing its few salient points together, is valuable as illustrative of what human existence is—a series of circles intersecting each other, but going on in a line. A few facts comprise man's life. A birth, a marriage, another birth, a baptism, a will, and then a funeral; and the old circle begins again.

Isaac is about to declare his last will. It is a solemn act in whatever light you view it, if it were only for the thought that we are writing words which will not be read till we are gone. But it is solemn too, because it is one of those acts which tell of the immortal. First, in the way of prophetic prescience. Is it not affecting to think of a human being, not sick, nor in pain, with his natural force unabated, calmly sitting down to make arrangements for what shall be when he is in his last long sleep? But the immortal is traceable in the act also, in that a dead man rules the world, as it were, long after his decease. Being dead, in a sense he yet speaketh. He is yet present with the living. His natural existence is protracted beyond its span. His will is law, a kind of evidence of his immortality; for the obedience of man to what he has willed is a sort of recognition of his present being.

Isaac was not left without warnings of his coming end. These warnings came in the shape of dimness of eyes and failing of sight. You can conceive a state in which man should have no warnings, and, instead of gradual decay, drop suddenly, without any intimation, into eternity; such an arrangement might have been. But God has in mercy provided reminders; for we sleep in this life of ours a charmed sleep which it is hard to break. And if the road were of unbroken smoothness, with no jolt or shock or unevenness in the journey, we should move swiftly on, nothing breaking that dead slumber till we awoke suddenly, like the rich man in the parable, in heaven or in hell "lifting up our eyes." Therefore God has given these reminders : some of them regular, such as failing of sight, falling out of hairs, decay of strength, loss of memory, which are as stations on the journey, telling us how far we have travelled; others irregular, such as come in the form of sickness, bereavement, pain; like sudden shocks which jolt, arouse, and waken. Then the man considers, and, like Isaac, says, "Behold, I am old, I know not the day of my death."

The chapter before us contains too much for one exposition; we will therefore take but the first portion of it, in which we find these two branches.

I. Isaac's preparation for death.

II. The united treachery of Jacob and Rebekah.

I. Isaac's preparation for death.

Here notice, first, his longing for the performance of Esau's filial kindness as for a last time. Esau was his favourite son ; not on account of any similarity between them, but just because they were dissimilar ; the repose and contemplativeness and inactivity of Isaac found a contrast in which it reposed in the energy and even the restlessness of his firstborn.

It was natural to yearn for the feast of his son's affection for the last time, for there is something peculiarly impressive in whatever is done for the last time. The simplest acts contract a kind of sacredness : the last walk in a country we are leaving ; the last time a dying man sees the sun set ; the last words of those from whom we have parted, which we treasure up as more than accidental, almost prophetic ; the last winding of a watch; the last act at night; the signature of a will. In the life of Him in whom we find every feeling which belongs to unperverted humanity the same desire to hallow a last act is found ; it is a trait therefore of the heart which is universal, and because universal, natural and right. "With desire I have desired to eat this passover with you before I suffer. *For* I say unto you, I will no more drink of the fruit of the vine till I drink it with you new, in My Father's kingdom." It was the *last* supper.

Secondly, Isaac prepared for death by making his last testamentary dispositions. They were made, though apparently premature, partly because of the frailty of life and the uncertainty whether there may be any to-morrow for that which is put off to-day ; partly perhaps because he desired to have all earthly thoughts done with and put away. Isaac lived thirty or forty years after this ; but he was a man set apart, like one who, in Roman Catholic language, has received extreme unction and has done with the world. And when he came to die there would be no anxieties about the disposition of property, to harass him. For it is good to have all such things done with before that hour comes. Is there not something incongruous in the presence of a lawyer in the death room, agitating the last hours?

The first portion of our lives is spent in learning the use of our senses and faculties, ascertaining where we are, and what. The second in using those powers, and acting in the given sphere, the motto being, "Work, the night cometh." A third portion, between active life and the grave, like the twilight between day and night, (not light enough for working, nor yet quite dark,) nature seems to accord for unworldliness and meditation. It is striking doubtless to see an old man, hale and vigorous to the last, dying at his work, like a warrior in armour. But natural feeling makes us wish perhaps that an interval might be given; a season for the statesman, such as that which Samuel had on laying aside the cares of office in the schools of the prophets, such as Simeon and Anna had for a life of devotion in the temple, such as the labourer has when, his long day's work done, he finds an asylum in the almshouse, such as our Church desires when she prays against sudden death; a season of interval in which to watch, and meditate, and wait.

II. The united treachery of Jacob and Rebekah.

It was treachery in both, in one sense the same treachery. Each deceived Isaac and overreached Esau. But it would be a coarse estimate to treat the two sins as identical. This is the coarse common way of judging. We label sins as by a catalogue. We judge of men by their acts; but it is far truer to say that we can only judge the acts by the man. You must understand the man before you can appreciate his deed. The same deed, done by two different persons, ceases to be the same. Abraham laughed, and so did Sarah : one was the laugh of scepticism, the other the result of that reaction in our nature by which the most solemn thoughts are balanced by a sense of strangeness, or even ludicrousness. The Pharisees asked a sign, in unbelief; many of the Old Testament saints, in faith A fine discrimination is therefore needed, to understand the simplest deed. A very delicate analysis of character is necessary to comprehend such acts as these and rightly apportion their turpitude and their palliations.

In Rebekah's case the root was ambition. But here is a trait of female character : it is a woman's ambition, not a man's. Rebekah desired nothing for herself, but for Jacob ; for him spiritual blessing, at all events temporal distinction : doing wrong, not for her own advantage, but for the sake of one she loved. It is a touch of womanhood.

The same is observable in her recklessness of personal consequences. So that only he might gain, she did not care : " upon me be thy curse, my son." And it is this which forces us, even while we most condemn, to compassionate. Throughout the whole of this revolting scene of deceit and fraud we never can forget that Rebekah was a mother ; hence a certain interest in and sympathy with her are sustained.

We mark another feminine trait; her act sprang from devotion to a person rather than to a principle. A man's idolatry is for an idea, a woman's for a person. A man suffers for a monarchy, a woman for a king. A man's martyrdom differs from a

woman's. Nay, even in their religion personality marks the
one, attachment to an idea or principle the other. Woman
adores God in His personality; man, in His attributes: at
least, that is on the whole the characteristic difference.

Now, here you see the idolatry of the woman, sacrificing
husband, elder son, principle, her own soul, for an idolized
person. Remark that this was, properly speaking, idolatry.
For in nothing is a greater mistake made than in the concep
tion attached to that word in reference to the affections. A
mother's affection is called by many religious people idolatry,
because it is intense. Do not mistake. No one ever loved
child, brother, sister, too much. It is not the intensity of
affection but its interference with truth and duty that makes it
idolatry. Rebekah loved her son more than truth, that is,
more than God. This was to idolize; and hence Christ says,
" If any man love father or mother more than Me, he is not
worthy of Me."

There are persons who would romantically admire this devotion of Rebekah, and call it beautiful. To sacrifice all, even
principle, for another; what higher proof of affection can there
be? O miserable sophistry ! The only true affection is that
which is subordinate to a higher. It has been truly said that in
those who love little love is a primary affection, a secondary one
in those who love much. Be sure he cannot love another
much, " who loves not honour more." For that higher affection
sustains and elevates the lower human one, casting round it a
glory which mere personal feeling could never give.

Compare, for instance, Rebekah's love with that of Abraham
for his son. Abraham was ready to sacrifice his son to duty ;

Rebekah sacrificed truth and duty to her son. Which loved a son the most? which was the nobler love? Even as a question of permanence, which would last the longer? For consider what respect this guilty son and guilty mother could retain for each other after this! Would not love dwindle into shame, and lose itself in recriminations? For affection will not long survive respect, however it may protract its life by effort.

Observe, again, monsters do not exist. When you hear of great criminality, you think of a nature as originally monstrous, not like that of others. But none are liars for the sake of lying. None love cruelty for cruelty's sake. It is simply want of principle which makes glaring sins. Best affections, noble ideas, perverted; that is the history of many crimes. See here. No touch of compunction from first to last. The woman is all unsexed. No thought of her defrauded eldest son, none of her deceived husband; inflexible pursuit of her object, that is all.

It is wonderful how ambition and passion dazzle men to all but the end desired. Wonderful how the true can become false, and the tenderhearted hard and cruel, for an end. Nor is this lesson obsolete. Are there no women who would do the same? None who would sacrifice a son's principles or a daughter's happiness to a diseased appetite for distinction? None who would conceal a son's extravagance, foster it, furnish it with means unknown to her husband, act in an underhand way in what is called the manœuvring of fashionable life, do that for family advancement from which the strong sense and principle of a father would revolt? And all this, not because they are monsters or demons, but because their passion for distinction is inflamed and their affections unregulated.

Secondly, look at Jacob's sin. He was not without ambition; but he had not that unscrupulous, inflexible will which generally accompanies ambition and makes it irresistible. A bad man naturally he was not; nor a false man; but simply a pliable and weak man. Hence he became the tool of another, the agent in a plan of villany which he had not the contrivance to originate. He was one of those who if they could would have what they wish innocently; he would not play false, and yet would unjustly win. He was more afraid of doing the deceit than anxious that the deceit should not be done. He had obtained the birthright and doubtless often longed for the blessing, though of himself he was not yet bad enough to form a plan like his mother's. It is from allowing ourselves to think of a forbidden thing that we get to long for it, and then gradually all obstacles in the attaining of it are taken away as soon as occasion presents itself. This is the history of all great crimes. Here was guilt in its germ. He had indulged and pampered the fancy; and be sure "he who wishes a temporal end for itself, does, or will soon, *will* the means." All temptations and all occasions of sin are powerless, except so far as they fall in with previous meditations upon the guilt; an act of sin is only a train long laid and fired by a spark at last. Jacob pondered over the desire of the blessing, dallied with it, and then—fell.

Now observe the rapidity and extent of the inward deterioration. See how this plain, simple man, Jacob, becomes by degrees an accomplished deceiver; how he shrinks at nothing; how, at first unable even to conceive the plan devised by another, he becomes at last inventive. At first the acted falsehood; he put on skins to appear hairy as his brother. Then the lie in so many words, " I am Esau thy firstborn"; then the impious use of the eternal Name, " the Lord thy God brought it me." See how he was *forced*, by fear and the necessities of begun guilt, into enormity deeper and deeper of guilt.

Happy the man who cannot, even from the faint shadows of his own experience, comprehend the desperate agony of such a state; the horror, mixed with hardening effrontery, with which a man feels himself compelled to take step after step, and is aware at last that he is drifting, drifting from the great shore of truth, like one carried out by the tide against his will, till he finds himself at last in a sea of falsehood; his whole life one great ocean of false appearance.

Apply this briefly. Doubtless, perverted good is always different from original vice. In his darkest wanderings, one in whom the Spirit strives is essentially different from one who is utterly depraved; sensibility to anguish makes the difference, even if there were nothing else. Jacob, lying in this way, plunging headlong deeper and deeper, was yet a different man from one who is through and through hollow. Grant this, and yet that fact of human pervertibility is an awful fact and mystery. Innocence may become depraved; delicate purity may pass into grossness; transparency of crystal clearness may end in craft, doubleness, contrivance : an appalling fact. Briefly, therefore :

First, learn to say No. Secondly, beware of those fancies, those day-dreams, which represent things as possible which should be for ever impossible. Beware of that affection which cares for your happiness more than for your honour. Lastly, in the hour of strong and terrible temptation, throwing ourselves off self, distrusting ourselves, let us rest in Him who, having been tempted, knows what temptation is; who will not suffer us to be tempted above that we are able, but will, with the temptation, also make a way to escape, that we may be able to bear it.

In the conclusion of this chapter two other personages remain, whose part in the transaction has to be examined : the deceived father, and the defrauded son and brother.

I. Isaac's conduct.

Remark, first, the double blessing : Jacob's containing temporal abundance, temporal rule, and spiritual blessing; the main points plainly being the rights of primogeniture. Esau's, in the first part identical with his brother's, but different afterwards by the want of spiritual blessing: God's gifts without God, the fruit of the earth and the plunder of the sword, but no connection with the covenant of God. Of course the destinies of Israel and Edom are prefigured in this, rather than the personal history of Jacob and Esau. For the predicted liberty of Edom, the breaking the yoke off the neck, did not take place till the reign of Jehoram, long after Esau's death (2 Kings viii. 22). So that when it is written, "Jacob have I loved, but Esau have I hated," the selection of nations to outward privileges is meant, not the irrespective election of individuals to eternal life.

Now in these blessings we have the principle of prophecy.

We cannot suppose that the Jacob here spoken of as blessed was unmixedly good, nor the Esau unmixedly evil. Nor can we imagine that idolatrous Israel was that in which all the promises of God found their end, or that Edom was the nation on whom the curse of God fell unmixed with any blessing. Prophecy takes individuals and nations as representations for the time being of principles which they only partially represent. They are the basis or substratum of an idea. For instance, Jacob, or Israel, represents the principle of good, the church of God, the triumphant and blessed principle. To that, the typical Israel, the promises are made; to the literal Jacob or Israel, only as the type of this, and so far as the nation actually was what it stood for. Esau is the worldly man, representing for the time the world. To that the rejection belongs, to the literal Esau only so far as he is that. In prophecies therefore, such as these, we are dealing much more with the ideas of which such persons and nations are the type than with the persons or nations themselves. And this will help us to understand why all the prophecies centre in Jesus Christ. In Him alone meet all those perfections of which others were the partial and fragmentary representations. The prophecy therefore, applied to them, is only partially true, because too grand for them. It represents them as perfect, which they were not, and only when they contain such perfection ensures the blessing to them. But Christ *is* that of which they were taken as representations, and to Him therefore belong the blessings. For instance the 53rd chapter of Isaiah was originally spoken of the Jewish nation, but only in a very limited sense could it be said of it that it had fulfilled the great idea of humanity—self sacrifice, or suffering whereby others are blessed. Only in the language of poetical hyperbole therefore is it true that Israel was wounded for our transgressions, and that Israel suffered as if the penalties of all nations were poured out on her. To make the prophecy reach its fulfilment, it must be applied to Him who *was* that which Israel's history only faintly shadowed.

So again, "Out of Egypt I have called My Son," words spoken by Hosea of the delivery of Israel from Egypt, but legitimately on this principle of interpretation applied by St. Matthew to Christ. All the magnificence of prophecy, limited to Israel, would be bombast; Christ alone fulfils the idea which Israel stood for.

Next observe Isaac's adherence to his promise.

If anything can excuse a departure from a promise, Isaac might have been excused in this case; for in truth he did not promise to Jacob, though Jacob stood before him. He honestly thought that he was speaking to his firstborn; and yet, perhaps partly taught to be punctiliously scrupulous by the rebuke he had received in early life from Abimelech, partly feeling that he had been but an instrument in God's hands, he felt that a mysterious and irrevocable sacredness belonged to his word once past, and said, "Yea, and he shall be blessed." Jesuitism amongst us has begun to tamper with the sacredness of a promise. Men change their creed and fancy themselves absolved from past promises; the member of the Church of Rome is no longer bound to do what the member of the Church of England stipulated. Just as well might the king refuse to perform the promises or pay the debts of the prince whom he once was. Therefore, let us ponder over such texts as these. Be careful and cautious of pledging yourself to anything; but the money you have once promised, the offer you have once made is irrevocable, it is no longer yours, it is passed from you as much as if it had been given.

II. Esau's conduct.

1. Remark his contentment with a second-rate blessing,— " Hast thou not another blessing?" etc. These words, taken by themselves, without reference to the character of him who spoke them, are neither good nor evil. Had Esau meant only this: God has many blessings, of various kinds; and looking round the circle of my resources I perceive a principle of com- pensation, so that what I lose in one department I gain in some other; I will be content to take a second blessing when I cannot have the first: Esau would have said nothing which was not praiseworthy and religious; he would have only ex- pressed what the Syro-Phœnician woman did, who observed that though in this world some have the advantages of children, whereas others are as little favoured as dogs, yet that the dogs have the compensatory crumbs.

This world of ours is built upon the principle of inequality. Its constitution is not democratical but aristocratical, not pres- byterian but episcopal. Nowhere do you find equality, every- where election, superior advantages in every department ; one born very rich, another with nothing; one slow of intellect, with narrow forehead, another with a capacious brain and large mind ; one surrounded by privileges which make it hard for him to miss the way of life, another seemingly excluded.

Now observe this is the principle of election, election to advantages, not election to spiritual happiness irrespective of character. For remember, superior advantages do not carry salvation nor moral superiority with them, necessarily ; nor do

H

inferior ones carry reprobation. Indeed, nothing is more beautiful than to see second-rate talents truly and conscientiously used ; to see, for instance, the slow boy toiling till he is equal to the gifted but less conscientious boy ; or the lonely soul rivalling the graces of one who is born with all that a church can do for him.

Now it was not in this spirit at all that Esau spoke. His was the complaining spirit of the man who repines because others are more favoured than he, the spirit of the elder son of the parable, " thou never gavest *me* a kid." *This* character transformed outward disadvantages into a real curse. For, again I say, disadvantages are in themselves only a means to more lustrous excellence. But if to inferior talents we add sloth, and to poverty envy and discontent, and to weakened health querulousness, then we have indeed ourselves converted non-election into reprobation ; and we are doubly cursed, cursed by inward as well as outward inferiority.

2. Remark Esau's malice (ver. 41). " The days of mourning for my father are at hand, then will I slay my brother Jacob."

Distinguish this from the resentment of righteous indignation. Resentment is an attribute of humanity in its original, primal state. He who cannot feel indignant at some kinds of wrong has not the mind of Christ. Remember the words with which He blighted pharisaism, words not spoken for effect but syllables of downright, genuine anger ; such expressions as peculiarly belong to the prophetic character, in which indignation blazes into a flame ; the prophetic writings are full of it.

Very different from this was Esau's resentment. Anger in him had passed into malice; private wrong had been brooded on till it had become revenge, deliberate and planned vindictiveness. Turn once more to the life of the Redeemer; you find scarcely a trace of resentment for injury done merely to Himself. Wrong and injustice He felt; but that it was done to Him added nothing to His feeling. The same He expounded as a principle in the parable. When Peter asked Him, "how oft shall my brother sin against me and I forgive him?" His reply was seventy times seven, an impossible number; and the reply contained a truth deeper and more beautiful than we venture to believe possible. It is this: that there is no injury which man can do to man which may not be forgiven and forgotten by one who has learned the lesson of love which is written in the blood of the cross.

Finally, observe the mixture of evil which taints the best characters. All the saints of God are exhibited to us with stains, often grievous ones. Here is Jacob, lying, defrauding, inventing treacheries. But let us not make too much of faults, errors, sins, crimes. We are all conscious of such things. Oh, yes! But the question is, what is the central life principle in us; one that will overwhelm them at last or not? You do not ask so much the amount of virus, of fever, which may be lodged in the constitution; but whether the constitution has strength to throw it off. Place these two men together, the man of the world and the man of God, and you would almost prefer Esau as certainly the more engaging character; but one had in him the seed of life, the other only feeling; and feeling like Esau's, without principle, is sure to dwindle at last like a plant without root. So you may lay in the earth an acorn and a bean beside each other; there is but a trifling difference between them; yet one will rise into the monarch of the forest, the other will never be more than a stunted vegetable. And the question for us is, not how many or how few faults, or evil acts, or vicious tendencies may be ours,—God knows they will not bear the counting; but is there in us, or not, a living germ which will develop—Christ in the heart, the Spirit of God within, the power of an endless life which will wither and at last cast out the evil?

One remark in application. Deeds are irrevocable; their consequences are knit up with them irrevocably. "Esau found no place of repentance, though he sought it carefully, with tears." Do not mistake that, as if it meant that Esau wishing to repent could not. No man ever desired the grace of repentance in vain. The very tears of Esau would disprove that. Had they been tears of sorrow, repentance was begun. Clearly, the repentance he sought for was his father's, not his own, repentance in the sense of change of purpose; and all his tears could not alter that purpose or change the word once passed. In a moment of passionate desire he had parted with his birthright, and now, having had his pleasure, he expected to have his blessing. He had sowed to the flesh, and expected to reap both the joys of the flesh and the peace of the spirit. This may not be. We reap as we have sown. He that sows, like Esau, to the flesh, reaps a harvest at first delicious, but it is soon over, and then he reaps corruption; but having had his harvest of present rapture, let him not complain if he finds that he has missed the harvest of spiritual peace.

LECTURE XV.

Sunday Afternoon, December 8, 1850.

GENESIS xxviii.

OUR subject for to-day is the journey of Jacob to Padan-Aram; but before we enter upon it we must make two preliminary observations. First, we are taught here the true evil of sin; it is not worldly but spiritual and moral loss. From that doubly treacherous act by which his father was beguiled and his brother defrauded, Jacob gained both the blessing and the patrimony; but what did he lose? Peace of mind, his father's trust, and his brother's love. Let us for one moment suppose that happiness should be the reward of sin, and misery the recompence of goodness; even then we would desire to do and to be good, not looking at the consequences, but bent on doing the good for its own sake, even though we were losers by so doing.

Secondly, we observe Rebekah's deep knowledge of human nature. Although Esau had so solemnly vowed vengeance, yet she knew that if Jacob absented himself for a time Esau would soon forget his resentment. The passionate, hasty man is not the one we need to fear; his rage will quickly spend itself in words. But the man to be feared is he who gives no sign of the war within, except perhaps by the blanched cheek or quivering lip; he will nurse his indignation, and it will burst forth in action.

In this journey of Jacob's the chief thing is his conversion which then took place. Jacob before this time was of the earth, earthy. From henceforth the character of his life is changed; new colours appear in his destiny. This was conversion. Conversion is the moment in life when the man becomes aware of a higher life beating within him, when from a natural he becomes a spiritual man. Now there are two ways of looking at conversion; some suppose that it is always sudden, while others look upon it as always gradual and slow; the truth lies between the two. It is sometimes sudden, as in the case of Jacob and also with Paul; but it is likewise gradual, as with John the Baptist, who from his mother's womb grew day by day in grace. Now in Jacob's conversion we must look at two things, first, the impressions made upon him, and secondly, the resolutions which he took.

I. Jacob's impressions.

These arose out of his journey. This, it is almost certain, was the first time of his leaving his father's home. Up to this he had been a plain man dwelling in tents. Probably he had not even slept from home, as the hunter his brother in that wild life of his, led far by the wild deer, must have done. Hitherto he had had little care, all was provided for him; but now, partly as the result of misconduct, partly because of parental arrangement, he sets out for a new land; probably, though grieved at the ties which were broken, yet enjoying the newness of the scene, for he was young and vigorous and the enterprise was being undertaken in the bright daylight. But when night came on, and there was no tent to repose under, and no pillow but a stone on which to lay his weary head, then a feeling of loneliness came over him, then tender thoughts awoke. He felt remorse, tears came unbidden. He felt, "I shall never be in my father's house the boy I was."

In all this observe: (1) A solemn conviction stealing over Jacob of what life is, a struggle which each man must make in self dependence. He is fairly afloat like a young swimmer, without corks, striking out for his life; dependent on self for defence, guidance, choice. Childhood is a time of dependence and thoughtlessness, and rightly so. How shall the child be fed, clothed, kept from contagion, cured? These things cause sleepless nights to parents; but childhood is oblivious of them; and this is wise, for life is a gradual development. The rosebud is protected by a green covering from the light; by expansion, by no rude shock, the bud passes into the blossom, flower, fruit. So it is with man. He passes from the state of dependence into that in which he must stand alone; but his growth differs from the flower's in this respect, that in his case the old is not broken off. His memory retains what has been. The past fades away from the mind of brutes: not so with man. Woe to him who forgets his home; woe, because he has no heart to work on. Man retains old links even when he gets new ones; the old are only less fettering. The time of independence comes. The boy is apprenticed, or the girl is married. It is a solemn crisis, because the way in which it is met often decides the character of the future life. Young children, confirmation tells you childhood is past, youth is here, manhood and womanhood are at hand; the ties of dependence are giving way; swathing bands, godparents, all are loosing; independence is at hand. You are launched. Now choose for yourselves. Self dependent, the boy must choose for himself, the girl for herself. But what is to direct their choice aright? What but the memory of what has been? The experiences of the past, these are to guide you.

(2) But beside this conviction of what life is, Jacob was impressed in another way at this time. God made a direct communication to his soul. "He lay down to sleep, and he dreamed." We know what dreams are. They are strange combinations of our waking thoughts in fanciful forms, and we may trace in Jacob's previous journey the groundwork of his dream. He looked up all day to heaven as he trudged along, the glorious expanse of an oriental sky was around him, a quivering trembling mass of blue; but he was alone, and, when the stars came out, melancholy sensations were his, such as youth frequently feels in autumn time. Deep questionings beset him. Time he felt was fleeting. Eternity, what was it? Life, what a mystery! And all this took form in his dream. Thus far all was natural; the supernatural in this dream was the manner in which God impressed it on his heart. Similar dreams we have often had; but the remembrance of them has faded away. Conversion is the impression made by circumstances, and that impression lasting for life; it is God the Spirit's work upon the soul.

(3) Jacob felt reconciliation with God. There is a distance between man and God. It is seen in the restlessness of men, in the estrangement which they feel from Him. Well, Jacob felt all this. He had sinned, overreached his brother, deceived his father. Self convicted he walked all day long; the

sky as brass; a solemn silence around him; no opening in the heaven; no sign nor voice from God; his own heart shut up by the sense of sin, unable to rise. Then came the dream in which he felt reconciliation with God. Do not mind the form but the substance. It contains three things: (i.) The ladder signifying heaven and earth joined, the gulf bridged over. (ii.) The angels signifying the communication which exists between earth and heaven. (iii.) The voice which told him of God's paternal care.

Now to us the ladder is Christ, and that in two ways. Christ bridges over heaven and earth by union of the human with the Divine, and by Him we have access to the Father. I say not Jacob saw this; but it is so to us, the ladder *to us* is Christ. Again, to us the angels *descending* are the intimations God gives us of His Spirit, the angels *ascending* are our prayers. Again, there is the voice speaking of fatherly protection, of hope, assurance to the end. This is made still clearer to us, for it is in Christ that we are made sons of God. Therefore conversion is seeing God in Christ, the habit of prayer, and the filial feeling towards God.

(4) The last impression made on Jacob was that of the awfulness of life. He exclaims: "Surely God is in this place; and I knew it not. And he was afraid, and said, How dreadful is this place! this is none other than the house of God and the gate of heaven" (ver. 16, 17). Children play away life. It is a touching and softening thing to see the child, without an aim or thought, playing away his young moments; but it is sad indeed to see men and women do this, for life is a solemn mystery, full of questions that we cannot answer. Whence come we? Whither go we?

How came we here? Say you that life is short, that it is a shadow, a dream, a vapour, a puff of air? yes, it is short, but it has an eternity wrapped up in it: it is a dream, but an awful, an appalling one, the most solemn dream of eternity that we shall ever have. Remember this is the gate of heaven, this is a dreadful place, the common is the Divine ; God is here. So Jacob felt, and therefore he made two resolutions.

II. The resolutions which he made.

The first of these was a resolution to set up a memorial of the impressions just made upon him. He erected a few stones, and called them Beth-el. They were a fixed point to remind him of the past. The power of this Beth-el we shall see when we come to read the 35th chapter. Herein is the value of forms ; impressions, feelings, will pass away unless we have some memorial. If we were merely spiritual beings, then we might do without forms ; but we are still mixed up with matter, and unless we have a form the spirit will die. Resolve then like Jacob to keep religion in mind by the use of religious rites. Churchgoing, the keeping of the sabbath, are not religion ; but religion hardly lives without them. If a man will say, I can read the Bible at home, think of Christ without attending the Holy Communion, make every day a sabbath, why, his religion will die out with his omission of the form. And this applies to those who are here candidates for confirmation. Be thankful and earnest in the acceptance of this rite, for experience tells how feelings fade. The world gets its cold hand on us, and sucks us down into its vortex. Therefore fix these sacred hours in your mind as a Beth-el; so that you may look back hereafter to resolves made now, in order to strengthen your life.

Secondly Jacob determined from this time to take the Lord for his God (ver. 21): "then shall the Lord be my God." He would worship from henceforth not the sun, or the moon, not honour, pleasure, business; but God. With respect to this determination, observe first: that it was done with a kind of selfish feeling; there was a sort of stipulation, that if God would be with him to protect and provide for him, that then he would take Him for his God (ver. 20, 21). And this is too much the way with us; there is mostly a selfishness in our first turning to God. A kind of bargain is struck. If religion makes me happy then I will be religious. God accepted this bargain in Jacob's case; He enriched him with cattle and goods in the land whither he went (chap. xxxi. 18): "for godliness has the promise of the life that now is." And this was the way in which the religion of the disciples arose; they put the question to Christ "What shall we have?" Disinterested religion comes later on. Afterwards the disciples thought no more of themselves but only of truth and their Master, and were willing to suffer martyrdom for His sake. And religion, so long as we live here, is a cross. We must count the cost of it beforehand, and not hope for material gain by it. Observe secondly what God *for our God* implies. It is not the mere repetition of so many words; for as our Lord has said, "Not every one that *saith* unto Me, Lord, Lord, shall enter into the kingdom of God." To have God for our God is not to prostrate the knee but the heart in adoration before Him. God is truth: to persist in truth at a loss to ourselves, that is to have God for our God. God is purity: resolve to shut up evil books, turn a countenance of offended purity to the insult of licentious conversation, banish thoughts that conjure up wicked imaginations; then you have God for your God. God is love: you are offended; and the world says, resent; God says, forgive. Can you forgive? Can you love your enemy, or one whose creed is different from your own? That is to have God for your God. God is infinite: to aim at goodness; aspiring on and on; ever higher, never satisfied; never expecting to reach perfection, but always longing after it; ever to aim at it, and die with it unattained. In a word, to follow and have Christ for your model, that is to have God for your God.

Lastly, applying this whole history to ourselves, we learn two lessons of life.

1. Jacob's faults were visited after conversion. He suffered a banishment of twenty-one years, and only returned in time to close his father's eyes. Fools say, I sin because I shall get off; but no man can escape the consequences of that which he has done. Repentance may give him a sense of pardon and take away the sting of remorse, but it cannot release him from the natural penalties of wrong doing.

2. See what life is! Trace this young hopeful heart on, until you see it before the prince of Egypt uttering these words: "Few and evil have the days of the years of my life been." Few! one hundred and thirty years! yet so it is even with all of us. Life before us looks long; life past a nothing. Moments linger; years fly. Life is short, therefore let us be up and doing. But his life had been "evil" besides. He

ad a sad retrospect: fourteen years of bondage; Rachel
everely won, then lost; then came a long widowhood in which
he saw a daughter disgraced, sons cruel, Joseph separated from
im, and a foreign home at last in the time of his grey hairs.
Such is life, not peace, but trial. Look on it calmly.
Expect nothing from the world, from the God of Jacob
everything.

LECTURE XVI.

Sunday Afternoon, December 15, 1850.

GENESIS xxix.

THE last chapter ended with a dream; this commences with a wearisome pilgrimage and a prosaic servitude of twenty-one years. Here is a lesson for life; God's extraordinary visitations are not frequent; they happen once or twice in a man's life, and then perhaps no more for ever. The remembrance however of them lasts during the long dull years of after life. Jacob did not forget this dream. So it was with Elijah; he was fed on angels' food, and on the strength of that went forty days in the wilderness. Once only was the glory of God seen on earth. It was at the transfiguration of our Lord, and from it the apostles received strength for their after life.

Our subject to-day will divide itself into two branches. First, Jacob's meeting with his relatives, and secondly, his servitude. In the first division there are three things for us to notice illustrative of New Testament modes of thought. First, we have an illustration of the Redeemer's thoughtfulness and care, as exemplified in the title of Shepherd. As Jacob drew nigh to Padan-aram, "he looked, and behold a well in the field, and lo, there were three flocks of sheep lying by it; for out of that well they watered the flocks: and a great stone was upon the well's mouth; and thither were all the flocks gathered" (ver. 2, 3). This is but a slight indication of all that these early shepherds were to their flocks, for in truth they were very different from what they are among us. The shepherds of that time looked upon their sheep as friends; they shared the same dangers as their sheep, and often risked their lives to procure sustenance for the sheep, and, as ever, danger intensified their mutual affection.

We have, secondly, a conception given to us of the church as a family. All had a right to move the stone from the well, and take water therefrom at any hour of the day; but they agreed only to open it once a day, and then take sufficient for the wants of the day (ver. 8), otherwise the well would have been left uncovered, for the stone was too heavy to be so frequently moved on and off for every one separately; and the consequence would have been that the well would have become impure and the water dried up. The family is the type both of the church and nation; and without the concessions, love, and consideration of a family, both church and nation lose their characteristic principles. Again, it is a unity of variety required to form a church, for so it is in the family; it is not composed of all brothers or all sisters, all parents or all children, but of all four united in their variety. Once more, there is this expression to be considered, "Surely thou art my bone and my flesh" (ver. 14). Manifestly here is the sacredness of family ties; Jacob had never seen Rachel before, but when he heard she was the daughter of Laban his mother's brother he felt drawn to her by a mysterious power, "and Jacob," we read, "kissed Rachel and lifted up his voice and wept" (ver. 11). Even so are Christians united to Christ and to one another in a spiritual manner.

We, secondly, pass on to consider the circumstances of Jacob's servitude. First, his agreement with Laban (ver. 18), "And Jacob loved Rachel, and said, I will serve thee seven years for Rachel thy younger daughter." We have here two things to notice; first, the degraded position in which women were regarded among the ancients. They were looked upon merely as slaves or servants; and therefore, as by marriage the father was deprived of his daughter's services, he always demanded some dowry or compensation; thus, Jacob served seven years to recompense Laban for the loss of his daughter's services.

We must next look at Laban's dishonesty in the non-fulfilment of his agreement. He says, in excuse, that it was not the custom of the country to give the younger before the elder (ver. 26). Perhaps not; but this is no palliation of his guilt, for he ought to have undeceived Jacob.

Once more, in this servitude of Jacob we find the principle of inevitable retribution. He had deceived his father, and here in his turn he was overreached. Leah deceived her husband, and in consequence lost his affection. Here both deceivers were justly punished. O my beloved brethren, be sure, be sure, be sure, your sin will find you out.

We have here, lastly, the principle of compensation; Leah lost her husband's affections, but she was blessed in her family (ver. 31). Here we have punishment tempered with mercy. This is what the cross has done for us; it prevents penalty from being simply penalty; it leaves us not alone to punishment, but mingles all with blessing and forgiveness. Through it life has its bright as well as its dark side.

LECTURE XVII.

Sunday Afternoon, December 22, 1850.

GENESIS xxxi. 48-50.

THE subject of this chapter divides itself into two branches :
first, Jacob's return (ver. 1-21) ; and, secondly, Laban's
pursuit (ver. 22-55).

I. Jacob's return.

Observe here that just as Jacob had begun to find himself
a home the voice of God was heard calling upon him to return
to his former country (ver. 3). The reason for this is manifest ;
it was intended to make him feel that he was but a stranger
and a pilgrim here, that this world was not his rest. And so
it is with us, every trial sent us is in order that we may not
make this world our home.

Observe also (ver. 19) Rachel's robbery of the images or tera-
phim, the household gods. These seem to have been in almost
general use among the Israelites. They were used for two
reasons : first for the purposes of divination and fortune telling ;
but secondly for the deeper reason of the insuperable tendency in human nature to worship God under a form. Wherein lay the guilt of this ? Not in worshipping God under a
form, for we cannot worship Him otherwise ; but in this—that
the form was necessarily inadequate and false, and therefore gave a false conception of God. There are but two forms
in which we, as Christians, are allowed to worship God ; to

I

worship Him through the universe, and through the humanity of Jesus Christ.

II. Laban's pursuit.

He complains of having been robbed, when he was really envious and suspicious (ver. 26, 27). We may be pretty sure of this, that when a man suspects another of being dishonest, over-reaching, or in any way impure, he is generally himself what he suspects others of being. Jacob here makes his defence; he is able to speak of his tender kindness, and also of his unswerving honesty (ver. 38-40). He had been a good and faithful servant to a bad master. And this is a lesson to the young, and to those in service. In the Catechism of the Church we say that our duty to our neighbour is to keep our hands from picking and stealing. Now *picking* is an old English word, and a very expressive one. There are many who would not steal a jewel, or break open a desk, and yet would take much smaller things, as a sheet of paper or a copper coin. The guilt of this is but very little different from that of stealing, though the temptation is smaller; and we may be sure that if they could not withstand that, they would not withstand a stronger temptation, especially if the way of escape was easy.

We lastly notice the covenant made between Jacob and Laban. They set up a heap and called it Mizpah, and said, "The Lord judge between me and thee" (ver. 49). Had this been the seal of friendship, it would have been most Christian; but it was made by enemies calling upon God to protect and defend them from each other's encroachments, as if they thought that God's sole purpose in the world was to make them happy individually and to avenge all their own little private wrongs, instead of ordering all things as shall most conduce to His own eternal glory and to their perfection.

LECTURE XVIII.

Sunday Afternoon, January 19, 1851.

GENESIS xxxii., xxxiii.

IN the last chapter we found Jacob escaping from Laban. This was done secretly, for he was in fear of the pursuit which really happened, the pretext for which was Rachel's having stolen her father's gods of gold. Laban's real motive, however, was a dread lest Jacob should become a dominant neighbour, a rival; and in order to prevent this taking place a covenant was made between them. Scarcely had Jacob escaped that danger when he encountered another : he had to pass through Mount Seir, where Esau had taken up his abode; and when the messengers that he had sent forward to his brother returned to him, and said that Esau was coming to meet him, then we read (ver. 7) that "Jacob was greatly afraid and distressed." This fear of his brother was the direct consequence of his sin, the sin that embittered his whole life. He only hears that his brother is at hand, and his heart at once sinks within him; the remembrance of his sin haunts him, the very mention of Esau's name brings it all fresh before him. Immediately before this a remarkable incident occurred; we read that the angels of God met him (chap. xxxi. 1). This is a passage which we cannot at present understand. Some commentators consider that the angels mean only the messengers of neighbouring kings; others look upon the passage as the record of a dream, and others again regard it as a real vision of heavenly visitants. The spiritual truth however which lies beneath the passage is at least clear, which is this; that Jacob here obtains a clear assurance of God's protection and guidance. We see therefore in him the union of two classes of feelings,—fear for the future, and trust in God ; and such must be ever our Christian life : not an entire life of rest, for we have sinned ; nor an entire life of unrest, for God has forgiven us : but in all life a mixture of the two. Christ alone had perfect peace, for He had perfect purity. If we would avoid this unrest we have but one remedy, sin not. For although the precious blood of Christ may cleanse us from the eternal guilt of sin, it will not take away its consequences here on earth.

The subject of these chapters is divided into two branches. First, Jacob's preparation for the meeting (chap. xxxii.) ; and, secondly, the meeting itself (chap. xxxiii.). His first preparation was a series of precautionary measures. He divides his flock into two bands ; he also arranges his family : first, his handmaids and their children, then Leah and hers, and lastly, his best beloved Rachel and Joseph. Those he cared least for he places first, in the front of the danger : the miserable question was whether he should lose all or those he loved least. Once more, all this anxious fear was the result of sin.

His next precaution was to send a present to Esau. In that he showed small knowledge of his brother's nature ; for Esau could not keep anger long, and had he kept his hatred so long, no present could have bought off the revenge that had been nursed for years.

The next preparation was Jacob's prayer; it was one of those prayers that rise out of the depths of a man's heart. There was, however, something in it that breathed of Jacob's character; there was a kind of selfishness in it. It is a dread of danger that has wrung that prayer from Jacob's lips. And yet allowance must be made for this, for our first prayer is ever this—a desire, not to be shielded from sin, but from temporal danger. The warrant upon which Jacob rested was true, it was on the goodness of God's character (ver. 9-12). He based his petition, not on any previous merits of his own nor on his own personal election. In times of danger considerations such as these will not hold good. God's character is eternal love ; what He is in Himself, and not what He is to us only, that is the ground of prayer. And this is what baptism teaches us, that we are God's children ; His paternity and our sonship, this alone can be the ground for prayer.

The next circumstance preparatory to the meeting was Jacob's wrestling with the angel. A something wrestled with him till break of day; at first it appeared as a man, then as an angel, and then as the infinite Jehovah Himself. This is a thing hard to be understood, for it tells of God almost overcome by His creature man. Moreover, that expressed desire to depart at break of day seems to tell of something supernatural, for it was an ancient belief that the spirits of the dead might wander in the night but were compelled to return before the first glimpses of the morning. But we cannot explain it away as a dream, for it was a positive fact that the sinew of the thigh shrank. Therefore the most honest and simple way is to confess that we cannot understand the historical fact : but this does not prevent our receiving the underlying spiritual truths; the truth of God's guidance and protection ; the truth that the struggle to know and to feel after God is the conflict of our whole life. Again, to the Hebrew, names meant truths and words were the symbols of realities; and this is the reason why the name of every place is so carefully given us. Jacob thus in desiring to know the name of God was desiring to know God Himself. And this is the question of questions, Is God but another name for nature, or is He not rather the Father of our Lord Jesus Christ? Although the name was not given, yet Jacob believed that God was with him ; and this leads us to the last spiritual truth, that out of these moments of struggle and doubt often comes our highest strength.

We pass on now to the consideration of chapter xxxiii., which contains the story of the meeting which ended in the reconciliation of the brothers. We first notice Esau's character ; he was truly generous, both in first refusing and then in receiving Jacob's present (ver. 9, 11); for if there were no one to receive, who could enjoy our Lord's blessing pronounced on those who give? He was generous too in the offer of an escort, and in his refusal to press it upon his brother (ver. 15). But in Jacob we see subtilty still (ver. 13, 14). Up to this time scarcely any act of his had been free from deceit; and for this sin he had all his life long to pay the price of fear and distrust and suspicion. The two brothers here proved the truth of our Lord's saying, " The Son of Man hath power *on earth* to forgive sins." The one forgave, and the other received his forgiveness, and went away with a feeling of absolution and peace. They soon parted, however, to meet no more for some years. In the separation perhaps they were wise, for although they had mutually forgiven yet confidence was lost. It is ever the consequence of sin, that perfect trust is afterwards impossible.

LECTURE XIX.

Sunday Afternoon, January 26, 1851.

GENESIS XXXV.

AT the close of the 33rd chapter we find Jacob, the wanderer, returned; his home once more has received him. And here the second period of his life begins. The first period was marked by success, the second was distinguished by bitter trials. We pass by the misfortunes, degradation, sin and troubles detailed in the 34th chapter; and we now fancy the much enduring man entering upon that portion of our existence when struggle and activity are exchanged for endurance and passiveness, with the shadow of the evil character of his sons darkening round his life. We take two subjects of thought from this chapter.

I. Refreshing of early recollections.

II. Gathering of misfortunes.

I. Refreshing of early recollections.

I use that word, refreshing, because we have here given us an account of Jacob's second journey to Bethel. His first visit is recorded in the 28th chapter, where we read of the vow that he made to serve God, and to make the pillar that he had erected God's house, if He would bring him back in peace to his father's house. It is rarely that such vows as these are performed in after life; in some cases it is impossible, in others the religious feeling which originally prompted them has fled.

Respecting this pilgrimage to Bethel, observe first, that it was done by Divine direction : "God said to Jacob, Arise go up to Bethel." Let us not imagine that a voice spoke articulately. There were simple modes of thinking in those days ; men had not learned to philosophize on their mental operations. They strongly felt an impulse within them. They knew that it was a higher one, and in the simple poetry of thought they said, God is speaking. The voice that spoke to Jacob was the voice within him, the voice of conscience, the same voice that speaks to us. Take the phrase " and God said" literally, and then we must believe that God spake to Jacob but does not speak to us, then we must look upon Him as a different God to us from what He was to Jacob : but no, He is the same. Oh, be sure of this. God is not extinct, but a living God ; His voice is now no more silent than in Jacob's time. If He seem silent, the fault lies in us, our ears are become dull of hearing, we want faith. Brother men, *believe* that God is present with us now, and then He is as much with us at Brighton as He was at Peniel.

Observe secondly, Jacob's preparation for this act of re-membrance. He puts away the strange gods from his house-hold. To confirm the naturalness of the narrative, refer to the earlier portion of the history, where we read of Rachel stealing the images of Laban for idolatrous worship. Of this Jacob at first appears not to have been cognizant, afterwards he was ; and when going to perform his vow, he puts away these idols. But wherein lay the evil ? Not in the use of forms and symbols, for these were afterwards given to the Jews by God. Idolatry consists in this ; the using of forms and images which give unnecessarily inadequate ideas of God, *unnecessarily* I say, for though all our notions are inadequate they ought not to be unnecessarily so. So Jacob buried the images under the oak. It was most wise. It was not sufficient to say, Let them not be worshipped, let the gold be kept merely for ornament. He knew human nature better; he knew that the same feeling would be suggested again whenever they were seen. And in our own day the things which have been the symbols of idolatry must be parted with. We may say that crucifixes and stone altars and lighted candles are nothing in themselves; but if they give the idea of localizing God, or in any way degrade His pure worship, then they must at once be buried. Happy for England is it that she has resolved to throw away all such things.

The third thing we remark here is the consecration of the place (ver. 1): "Make there an altar to God, that appeared unto thee when thou fleddest from Esau thy brother." And this is the real meaning of consecration. It is not to make God more in one place than another. That is impossible, we cannot bind the Infinite. But the object is this : to appeal to our nature to enable us to feel God more profoundly in one place, and so to make us feel Him more surely in all places. It is not then in reference to Him, but for a help to our own feelings that we consecrate certain spots of earth and buildings. And so it was with Jacob. He was not to go to Bethel and set up an altar to make God there more, but to feel by association more deeply that He was there.

In all this there is indisputable truth. There are sacred

places, not sacred for their own sake, but sacred to us. Where we have loved and lost, where we have gained new light and life, the church where our forefathers worshipped, the place where we first knew God—these are by instinct hallowed. Hence we are told that God met Jacob in Bethel; not that He came down from another place, for He is everywhere, but that Jacob experienced a feeling of awe, a feeling that God was then specially near to him.

In this meeting of Jacob with God, there are two facts to observe. The first is that since he was last at Bethel he had increased in the knowledge of God. He knew Him then only as God, now he knows Him as the God Almighty (ver. 11). This is but a type of our own life ; our knowledge of God must always be progressive. Another thing we perceive, that in these twenty years there had been a growth in his personal religion. Once it had been but a selfish religion : he adopted a system of barter with God ; if God will give me bread to eat and raiment to put on, then shall God be my God (chap. xxix.). Now there is a higher step, it is gratitude ; God has done it, and now God shall be his God (ver. 3) : a higher motive, but not the highest ; he has yet to learn to serve Him, not in happiness but in misery ; to serve Him in trial, because He is God, and to learn to say simply and believingly, Thy will be done. We pass on now to consider—

II. The gathering of his misfortunes.

The first of these was one not so keenly felt, the death of Deborah, Rebekah's nurse. He buried her at Bethel, under an oak (ver. 8) ; and the story gives us an interesting view of the ancient relation between master and servant. It was not one f slavery or lucre, but of attachment; faithful service was given in return for generous protection. This death was Jacob's first blow. It did not fall on him severely. It did not touch him to the quick, for it was natural and regular; in the course of nature the ancient servant had died full of years. It is only those griefs which are the consequences of our misdoings which are almost insupportable trials. But Jacob's second blow was of a different kind: Rachel dies, his early and youthful passion, his beloved wife; the only one whom with all his strength of affection Jacob loved, and whose children were dearer for her sake to him than all the others. Even his father and fondly indulgent self-sacrificing mother he seems to have regarded with coldness. From this moment he becomes a mourner for the rest of his life; and yet we can see the infinite good of this. Jacob was a selfish, comfort-loving man; these sorrows drew him out of himself to think of something higher. The last blow was the death of Isaac (ver. 29). The brothers met over their father's grave, but the reconciliation was but outward; sin had separated them, and though Esau might trust Jacob, Jacob could never have trusted Esau whom he had so deceived. This death of Isaac was natural too, yet solemn, because it brought home the thought of death to Jacob; Deborah was, as it were, two generations back, and Rachel's death was sudden, out of the natural course; but when Isaac was gone, Jacob must have felt that he stood at the head of the present generation, marked out now to receive the first blow of death.

LECTURE XX.

Sunday Afternoon, February 2, 1851.

"And Isaac gave up the ghost, and died, and was gathered unto his people, being old and full of days: and his sons Esau and Jacob buried him."—GENESIS XXXV. 29.

WE have all heard of the first disagreement between the two brothers, Esau and Jacob; a disagreement which had the effect of severing them, under circumstances of great bitterness, for some years, but which had at length ended, as we read in the 33rd chapter of this book, in a reconciliation. And now we find the two brothers, who had taken up their abode, the one at Bethel in the land of Canaan, and the other at Mount Seir in the land of Edom, meeting in peace and brotherly kindness for the burial of Isaac their father; even as Isaac and Ishmael had met, under circumstances not altogether unlike, to bury Abraham their father in the self-same spot, the **cave** in the field of Machpelah before Mamre (xxv. 9).

There is a holy lesson to be learned from this narrative, which stands in pleasing contrast to the melancholy history of craft on one side and unforgivingness on the other between the two brothers. The change in Esau is especially worthy of observation. He had said in his heart, some forty or fifty years before: "The days of mourning for my father are at hand; then will I slay my brother Jacob." And yet at their next meeting, which cost Jacob so much fear and anxiety before

t took place, which brought him on his knees in prayer and
earnest supplication to God, it was Esau, the injured brother,
who "ran to meet the supplanter Jacob, and embraced him,
and fell on his neck, and kissed him." Nor were Jacob's
words less touching—evidencing, as they do, his humiliation in
being thus lovingly greeted by the brother he had wronged :
" Nay, I pray thee, if now I have found grace in thy sight,
then receive my present at my hand : for therefore I have seen
thy face, as though I had seen the face of God, and thou
wast pleased with me." And now they had met again by
their father's grave in peace !

What a lesson to brothers that separate in wrath, and cherish
their anger for years, and are proud and moody and unreason-
able, saying their daily prayer without a meaning ! What a
lesson to many between whom the petty and miserable strifes
which ensue about small affairs have produced, I fear, enduring enmities ! We hear that such and such persons are
not on terms, as it is called ; and when we ask why, the
wretched reason is that, in a division of property, one got
the better of the other ; or that, in a struggle of parties, one
took the one side, the other the other, and a chance word
kindled a fire. What a lesson to Christians ! We see that
those who lived under the elder dispensation could arrange
their feuds ; but we, who have seen Christ crucified, who owe
our only hope of forgiveness to His pardoning love, cherish
our enmities in our breasts, dwell on them for years, let them
burst forth on every occasion, carry our strife about with us
wherever we go, lay it not down even in God's house, suffer it
to keep us from the Holy Communion for years, or smother it

and stifle it while we prepare ourselves for that sacrament, to let it break forth again when we next meet our adversary face to face! And each party, if you plead with them, will tell you they have no ill feeling, it is the other who is angry, they say : just as Adam, our forefather, summoned to account, said, "It was the woman." Ay, but as both the man and the woman and all their descendants suffered from that fault in both, so in every quarrel among brethren do the quarrellers and all connected with them, and the community to which they belong, suffer loss !

Oh, let us visit the field of Machpelah, seek the cave where Esau and Jacob are laying the body of Isaac—those two brothers, in whose boyhood the seed of their future separation was sown by the foolish partiality of the mother for her younger son, the quiet home-loving boy, by the favouritism of the father for his fine, bold, intrepid hunter lad, whose venison he ate while he loved to hear him tell of the dangers of the chase. Let us behold them, both bearing on their visage the marks of labour and sorrow gone through since those early days : Esau, the man of strength, in war now as in the chase of old living by the sword; Jacob, the breeder of sheep and cattle, whom for twenty years the drought consumed by day, the frost by night, and sleeplessness and anxious care ! And him God had taught as He doth ever teach those whom He loves ; had bowed his neck under the yoke, had chastened and afflicted him and brought his sin to remembrance. The death of Rachel, the sin of Reuben, the violence and wrath of Simeon and Levi of whom Jacob prophesied and said, "Cursed be their anger,

or it was fierce ; and their wrath, for it was cruel"—all this
lay heavy upon the heart of Jacob. He was an altered
man, no doubt, from the day when he entered into the
presence of his father, with the dressed kid in his hands and
the wine, and the goodly raiment of Esau upon his shoulders,
a deceiver, a supplanter, rightly named Jacob, though now
Israel, even "one who had power with God and prevailed."
There they stood by their father's grave; the twins that had
struggled together in the womb, an omen of a future and a
fiercer struggle in the trials of life.

What a lesson! What a reality! A type and figure of
trials, strifes, struggles, differences, jealousies, and evils ensuing from these, in all ages, to the end of the world. But,
thank God, a type also of reconciliations, concessions, repara-
tions, an encouragement to piety and to paying due honour
to a parent's memory! And as such, let us hope, not recorded in vain.

How the scenes of their childhood must have recurred to
them, as they saw the body of their father laid by the side of
his father Abraham! Both must have been thinking of the
same thing; of the day when Esau came in faint and weary
from hunting, and would fain give his birthright in exchange
for the pottage which Jacob had prepared. But they thought
also of all that had followed and the things that might be yet.

Esau's thoughts went away from his birthright, and God's
favour and blessing, to the cities and fortresses he had built,
to his wives and children in Seir,—those that had been a grief
of mind to Isaac and Rebekah—to her whom he had married
afterwards in deference to their wishes, Bashemath, the

K

daughter of Ishmael—even to them and to his childre[n] whom he himself had deprived of their blessing.

Jacob thought upon the birthright, the promise where[of] was renewed to him at Bethel, and which now by the deat[h] of his father had devolved on him as the seed to whom i[t] belonged ; an inheritance still future, a possession still t[o] come ; not his, but rather his children's after him, when in hi[s] seed all families of the earth were to be blessed. And this [of] itself would carry his thoughts backward and onward, awa[y] from present things ; first perhaps to Rachel's grave, an[d] Benjamin, the son of his right hand, yea, Benoni, son of h[is] sorrow ; and then on and on, to things yet in the womb [of] time, perhaps beyond all time. Should he see Rachel y[et] again ? What did this blessing, which now centred in hi[m] and his, what did it mean ?

We have no clue to his thoughts but the hopes and aspir[a]tions of that common nature which are called forth by trials an[d] circumstances, which we have still in common with those wh[o] have gone before us in the generations. But this is a clue whic[h] we may surely follow, and which we may follow to our benef[it] if we let it lead us onward from a more faithful and earne[st] discharge of our daily duties, especially of filial and fratern[al] duty, to the day when whatsoever good thing any man dot[h] the same shall he receive of the Lord, whether he be bond [or] free, high or low, rich or poor ; when the son who honoure[s] his father and mother, either by paying them all deference an[d] respect, or by supporting them in poverty, or by upholdin[g] them in their infirmity, or by paying the last tribute of affectio[n] and respect to their remains, shall so also himself receive [of]

he Lord; or when the brother, who came to his brother
vhom he had injured or who had injured him, with blessing
nd forgiveness on his tongue, shall in like manner hear his
wn forgiveness fully accorded by Him who is over all;
vhen the duteous daughter or loving sister shall inherit the
eward of patient and constant love in the everlasting glory.
Vhen, as we know, (and, it may be, Jacob foresaw even if Esau
:new it not,) we shall meet again in a better country—father,
nother, brethren, sisters, children, wife, or husband—when
acob and Rachel shall be reunited, and the blessing that was
promised to the descendants of Abraham shall be fulfilled to
heir spiritual seed, to all who have lived and died in the faith
f Christ.

These are the common lessons of every funeral, when the
ope of faith is not darkened by misdeeds, or blighted
y estrangements or offences. Who ever saw the last
ickering of the spark of life, or heard the sound of the
andful of dust cast down into the grave, who did not wish
om his heart that the evil word had never been spoken, the
vil thought never entertained, the evil deed never done, the
vil concupiscence never indulged, the evil never repaid
ith evil; that the intercourse of life had been carried on in
ve, and the dealings of the world sweetened all along by
mutual forbearance and gentleness? Who doth not wish it,
ng for it? Alas! we cannot pray for it; for even prayer
vails not to undo the past. But who would not then forego
ll he ever gained, if he might be again as he was in the days
f his youth, whenever he thinks of some ungentle, unkind,
nforgiving, undutiful, unseemly act of later life? If over

the grave of an Isaac or an Esau such thoughts hav
arisen in the heart of one who hath been what Jacob wa
to them, let him remember, that to supplant or to deceiv
is a bitter root, and must trouble a man all his after day
But to forgive and be forgiven is a blessedness to be attaine
only while life lasts, while hand can clasp hand, and ey
beam on eye, and words of kindness be interchanged! Th
grave closeth, stilleth all in silence never to be broken, sav
in empty dreams and idle wishes poured forth ever afterwar
in vain. Therefore let us take heed betimes, while kin
and pleasant offices can still be interchanged and life an
its varied interests continue, that we may call forth the heart
best affections, that we may kindle zeal and fervour in ou
soul toward our fellow men; for a day of gloom succeedet
in which there is no longer space for these dispositions
grow.

Yet another thought connects itself with the death of Isaa
who thus "died, and was gathered unto his people, being ol
and full of days"; and that is the simple thought of his ente
ing into the rest that remaineth for the people of God. Aft
a long, and in some respects a prosperous life—though h
was not without his share of anxiety and sorrow—he quiet
sank into the grave. He had seen the reconciliation of h
children, and had doubtless acquiesced in the fulfilment of th
prophecy spoken when they were yet in the womb, that "th
elder should serve the younger." It is evident from his wor
to Jacob when he sent him to Padan-Aram that he believe
the blessing of Abraham would descend in the line of th
posterity of Jacob his younger son. And in this belief th

rk of his life was ended. According to the words of
iphaz in the Book of Job, he knew that "his seed should
 great; and his offspring as the grass of the earth. And
 came to his grave in a full age, like as a shock of corn
meth in his season."

My brethren, what exchange hath life for such a death?
ore especially when the strength that remaineth to man is
t labour and sorrow; when the knees are feeble, and the
ep is slow and faltering, and the flesh dried up for want of
tness. There be some whom we meet in our daily walk, in
hose very countenances we read the story of a long and
eary pilgrimage; whose eye seems to ask, "What is my
rength that I should hope; and what is mine end, that I
ould prolong my life?" They do but wait the days of their
pointed time till their change come; happy when they
all be gathered unto their people, as Isaac was, in Isaac's
mple faith, who, while he dwelt in tabernacles in a strange
nd, "looked for a city which hath foundations, whose Builder
d Maker was God."

We must not indeed suppose that mere weariness of this
e is an earnest of that rest, nor suffering and want and
rdship in this world a title to future glory. But the strong
stincts of our nature are not to be repressed, and the words
 the son of Sirach are true: "O death, acceptable is thy
ntence unto the needy, and unto him whose strength faileth,
at is now in the last age, and is vexed with all things."
nly let us labour that when the stroke comes we may be
epared to meet it, that it may find us in a state of repent-
ce toward God and faith toward our Lord Jesus Christ—

engaged in lawful and pious works, having our hearts fixed
a better country, that is, an heavenly! Are we at variance wi
any, especially with any of our own kindred, with brother
sister? Let us remember that to be at peace with all men
one of the chiefest and most fitting preparations for a tra
quil and happy death. Have we wronged any one? Let
express at least our sorrow. Have we suffered wrong? L
us at least forgive all that have injured us. And if our pri
of heart rebel against the effort, let us meditate on the sce
exhibited to our view in the words of the text, where tw
brothers, whose cause of quarrel was no ordinary disagre
ment, (for could Jacob have made any adequate compensati
to Esau for the blessing of which he had deprived him
where, I say, two such men stood side by side at the
father's grave, and forgot, in the remembrance of their chi
hood and their present grief, all but the performance of th
last duties to him who gave them birth.

LECTURE XXI.

Sunday Afternoon, February 9, 1851.

GENESIS xxxvii.

AT the beginning of this chapter we read, "These are the generations of Jacob" (ver. 2). In the last chapter those of Esau are briefly mentioned, and from this time we hear no more of him or his descendants, except as they come across the path of Israel's history, or as they are brought out in the page of prophecy to stand as a beacon to the world. This practice of following out one family is most evident throughout the Book of Genesis. We read of Abraham and his two sons ; the history of Isaac is taken up and we scarcely hear of Ishmael ; again, the history of Jacob is continued while we hear no more of Esau; and again, with Jacob's family, Joseph is the one chosen out of all the sons, his history alone is brought before us and we know little more of all the rest. And this division observable in the Jewish nation is but a type of what is going on in this world ; there are two sides, those which may broadly be classed as the good and the bad. There has ever been the World, with the Church existing as a protest against it. And the lesson for us to learn here is that in every act and conversation there are two sides, and that in everything we do or say we are deciding our place, as to which of these sides we belong to. Now this chapter divides itself into two branches.

I. The division found in Jacob's family.

II. The mission of Joseph to Shechem.

I. The division found in Jacob's family. In the very outset of the chapter we find that Jacob's was a divided family ; and for this division we find four reasons. The first is the favouritism with which Jacob had loved Joseph (ver. 3). In God's government there is election, but no favouritism ; for God judges by character. But turning to the conduct of Jacob, we find something different. True, Joseph was superior to his brethren, but there was something more ; he was the son of the favourite wife and therefore the favourite child. His coat was the badge of his father's unjust love, and therefore upon it his brethren wreaked their fury.

The principle which we extract from this is a simple one : in the government of the nation or the family undue or unjust favouritism leads to dissension.

The second cause for this division was the scandal-bearing of Joseph (ver. 2). The youth, so good and pure in other respects, descended to the office of a talebearer ; behind his brothers' backs the tale was told ; he who should have shielded their character from shame was the first to reveal their ill doings. Charity, it is said, covereth, that is, casts a veil over, a multitude of sins. Now the church of Christ is a family ; and yet this love of evil report still lives amongst us. It is not, however, true to say that no evil is to be said of man, for then there would be no such thing as character ; but you must draw the distinction between the accusation openly made and that which is brought in secret. The Christian man who sets himself to the duty of the public informer has got a miserable task ; but quite distinct from this is the spirit which, with the tongue of a brother and the heart of an enemy, wounds in secret, the spirit which carries evil report from house to house. And yet perhaps in the midst of such a conversation there is no one syllable on which we can fasten and say that slander has been uttered. It is done by a look, by the uttering of such sentences as these : " Indeed ! You don't say so ! I could not have believed it !" It is in this way that the family of Christians is split into infinite divisions.

The third reason for this division was the polygamy of Jacob. Now let it be remembered that in those days there was no law against polygamy, and therefore in that act there was no sin ; for, says the apostle, "sin is not imputed where there is no law." And yet you will observe that, though this was no sin in Jacob, yet that the penalty followed, for it was against the constitution of God's world ; still, as it was not in contradiction to any revealed law, his conscience was not defiled ; it was but penalty, not chastisement. The laws of God are not arbitrary ; They are the provision of a Father's love to protect us from the consequences of evil ; it is the love of God that says to us, " Sin not."

The last reason for this division was the envy of the brothers; Joseph told his dreams, and these made them hate and envy him. Now we distinguish between two things, jealousy and envy. Jealousy is that state of mind which repines at the happiness of another, the diminution of which would increase our own. Envy, on the contrary, is that state of mind in which we mourn over the advantage of another, though the taking it away from them will not do us the least good. Envy is that terrible state in which it is impossible to admire anything that is not our own. We can pardon the jealousy of the poor man who repines over the advantages wrung from him by the false customs of society; but we cannot sympathise with him when he hates all that is above him simply because it is above him.

II. Joseph's mission to Shechem. Jacob sent him to see how his brethren fared. When they saw him coming, they resolved at first to slay him; but, as it were by accident, a party of Ishmaelites were there, to whom they sold their brother into slavery. Observe here the bloodguiltiness of these brothers; they did not take Joseph's life, but they intended to take it; they were therefore murderers. Let us make a distinction; for when we are told that the thought is as bad as the crime, sometimes we are tempted to argue thus,—I have indulged the thought, I will therefore do the deed, it will be no worse. This sophistry can scarcely deceive the heart that uses it; yet, merely to put the thing verbally right, let us strip it of its casuistry. The thought is as bad as the act, *because* the act would be committed if it could. But if these brethren of Joseph had mourned over and repented of their sin, would we dare to say that the thought would have been as bad as the act? But we do say that the thought in this case *was* as bad as the act, because it was not restrained or prevented by any regret or repentant feeling; it was merely prevented by the coming in of another passion, it was the triumph of avarice over malice. There is many a man who has not taken away a brother's life, but who, by an indulgence of malevolence, is in the sight of God a more sinful man than many who have expiated their guilt on the scaffold.

But all these brothers were not equally guilty. Simeon and Levi and others wished to slay Joseph; Judah proposed his being sold into captivity; while Reuben tried to save him secretly, although he had not courage to save him openly. He proposed that he should be put into the pit, intending to take him out when the others were not by. His conduct in this instance was just in accordance with his character, which seems to have been remarkable for a certain softness. He did not dare to shed his brother's blood, neither did he dare manfully to save him. He was not cruel, simply because he was guilty of a different class of sin. It is well for us, before we take credit to ourselves for being free from that or this sin, to inquire whether it be banished by grace or only by another sin. You are not censorious, but then pause and ask whether you are not too lax to be censorious : you are not a talebearer or a busybody, but are you certain that you have in you sufficient love for others to make you at all interested in their matters? It is thus very possible for devils to be cast out by Beelzebub, the prince of the devils. Observe too the calmness of these men after their crime ; they sat down by the pit to eat and to drink (ver. 24). We often think respecting the tyrants of whom we read in history, that they must have been haunted by the Furies. Brethren, it is not so, there is a worse doom for sin than this ; it is that it makes the heart callous and forgetful of its presence. If there were but the sting it would be well, for it would lead to reformation.

LECTURE XXII.

Sunday Afternoon, February 16, 1851.

GENESIS xxxix., xl.

IN the close of the 39th chapter we find Joseph in an Egyptian prison; he had been tried, tempted, chastened, and come off the purer and the stronger. The disappointed passion of Potiphar's wife had settled down into malice. There are two kinds of love: that love which ever increases, and that which, usurping the name of love, contains within itself the germ of its own destruction.

In the account of Joseph's imprisonment is given to us an explanation of one of the mysteries of this our human life. It is a mystery that often sinfulness and selfishness reap the prizes here, while goodness and integrity have to endure the ills of this life. Looking on this in our infinite ignorance we are sometimes inclined to say that it is not justice, but chance, that rules this world; or, in our infinite wisdom, we say that this world is a state of probation, and that, although we suffer here for well doing, yet that in the world to come we shall have happiness and peace; as if the introduction of the element of time could make any difference; as if that which it would be unjust to do in eternity would not be so now. Now I ask you to observe the utter falseness of this solution. It is as if we thought that the Everlasting rewarded the goodness of His servants as a foolish mother giving her child that which is pleasant to the taste. We do well, and suffer for it; and then we complain that we have not our reward in material prosperity. In this history we have an illustration that bears on the question. Shortly after his imprisonment, Joseph was released, his merit acknowledged, and almost regal dignity conferred upon him. Whereupon we say, " Now all is right, merit has its reward "; and with this poetical justice we are satisfied. But this is not the justice of God's world. Are these then the rewards of well doing—horses and carriages, the royal robe, and the knee bowed before him ? Is it with these things, quite earthly, that the Everlasting rewards celestial qualities ? Brethren, neither in this world nor in the world to come are these the rewards of goodness. What was Joseph's reward ? Not the rank conferred upon him ; but this— to be pure, to be haunted by no principle of remorse. It is written in the sermon on the mount, "Blessed are the pure in heart, for they shall see God." To see God, to have the vision of the King in His beauty, to know and to feel that He is near—that was Joseph's reward. And think you that, from this, the dungeon could take much ; and that, to this, his earthly honours could add anything? The reward of well doing is God ; and what could be added to a prize so glorious ?

In these chapters we shall briefly go through three or four unconnected points.

First. Joseph's rising favour with the keeper of the prison (chap. xxxix. 22, 23). We observe here the real nature of human influence. It is not the influence of rank, but of character. Make all men equal in rank to-day, and to-morrow there will be found those who have acquired influence over the others. These prisoners were all in the same position, but very soon Joseph's character gained him influence. Thus, by the influence of Paul, the jailer at Philippi was converted, Felix trembled before him, and Agrippa was almost persuaded to be a Christian. Let such a man be imprisoned, but he will soon have converted Cæsar's household, for his influence is real.

Again observe the religious tone of this account. We read nothing of Joseph's intellectual superiority, but that " the Lord was with him " (ver. 21). The reason of his influence was the God within him. Just so far as a man is Christlike will he have influence.

We next observe the channel by which God so often chose to manifest Himself to His servants—through dreams. Dreams are the presentation in sleep of certain impressions made in our waking hours. In our waking thoughts, will is active ; in our sleeping thoughts, will is dormant. It was natural, both as a fact and as a belief in those early times, that these should be the moments chosen by the Spirit of God to reveal Himself to His servants. When the will of man ceased, then naturally was the time for God to choose to make known His will, for the Everlasting Spirit to mix itself with the finite and temporal spirit.

We observe also the characteristic nature of those dreams. In every case the dream betrayed the man. In the 40th chapter we find the record of two dreams, that of the butler and that of the baker. The butler dreamed of three great vine branches and ripe grapes, the baker of three baskets of baked meats ; and Joseph, in one of his own dreams, dreamt of agriculture, the calling to which he had been accustomed. The application that we make of this is, that our sponta- neous thoughts betray our character. The trivial man dreams of trivial things; but if the vision that is presented is to a man like St. Paul, he is lifted up to the third heaven and hears unutterable things which it is not lawful to speak. The dream itself is evidence of a man of deep feeling and imagination, and of a life of spirituality. When Peter too dreamed of the sheet let down from heaven and was told to kill and eat, he says, "Not so, Lord; for I have never eaten anything common or unclean." The answer speaks of a long life of obedience, for even in his dream he could not be induced to transgress the written law of God. In our hours of contem- plation the soul is surrounded by its own creations; and if they be of a holy character, the man lives as in the presence of God and angels; but if, on the contrary, instead of imagination spiritualized and purified, the spirit is but sensualized, the man has then made for himself his own hell.

We have now three things to observe in Joseph's conduct: First. The tenderness of his sympathy; he observed the shade on the countenances of his fellow prisoners, and imme- diately asked why they were sad (ver. 6, 7). This tenderness of feeling was gained only by suffering. Joseph had suffered like them, and therefore he understood their feelings. With the value of suffering we are familiar; but we do not often remember that suffering is absolutely necessary to capacitate us for sympathy. Would you be a Barnabas, a son of con- solation? Brother men, you may; but then you must pay the cost, the education of the soul by suffering.

The next thing we observe of his conduct in the dungeon is the profession of his innocence, of which notice the calmness and simplicity (ver. 15). " For indeed I was stolen away out of the land of the Hebrews, and here also have I done nothing that they should put me into the dungeon." There are no invectives against his brethren, or against Potiphar and his wife; he merely states that he was innocent. Calm assertion is *generally* a proof of innocence. When you hear men cursing and swearing, like Peter, in order to asseverate their innocence, you may feel assured that there is guilt. It has been well observed, that this calmness of speech in the gospel history is an evidence of its truth. Had it been a fiction, how would the writer have enlarged on the injustice of the Jews, and the difference in the characters of the blessed Redeemer and Barabbas! whereas the evangelist makes no comment, but simply and calmly states the fact,—" now Barabbas was a robber."

The last thing we observe in Joseph's conduct is the integrity of his truthfulness. It was a pleasant thing to tell the chief butler that he should be reinstated in his office ; but it was not pleasant to tell the baker that after three days he should be hanged. Yet Joseph could not shrink ; having once accepted the office of interpreter he was obliged to fulfil it faithfully. This truthfulness was a matter of habit as well as of principle with Joseph. There are many men who would not tell a direct falsehood, and yet their ordinary habit is by no means strictly veracious. With no distinct intention of doing wrong, they embellish and exaggerate. Therefore, let us get the habit of accuracy ; and when a thing is simply *unpleasant*, let us not say that it is *dreadful*. These are merely habits ; but by degrees they break down the truth of the Christian character.

Lastly, in this dungeon scene we find a striking similarity to the dying hour of Christ,—one innocent between two male- factors ; and in each case one guilty one was pardoned and the other condemned. It is not merely to show the similarity that we notice this fact, for we do not approve the habit which by fastening the mind upon the letter of Scripture loses its spirit ; but we quote it as an illustration of the truth with which we com- menced. Jesus and the malefactors suffered the same death ; and then this difficulty arises to many minds, There is one end to all ; or, as Solomon expresses it, "All things come alike to all." Brethren, it is only in a man's Epicurean moments that he dares to say a thing like that. All things come *not* alike to all. It was the mere similarity of the outward circumstances of that dungeon that made the lot of Joseph like that of those who were with him. His mind being free, the dungeon could scarcely impair that liberty. Was the end of the Redeemer similar to the end of those malefactors ? Some Christian writers have dared to say that for the redemption of the human race,—I almost shrink from saying it,—that for one hour the soul of the Redeemer was in hell ! Do they know what hell is ? Hell is the remorse of doing wrong. To have felt that would have been to have blotted out God from the world. There was the infinite agony we cannot comprehend, that of infinite Purity suffering ; there was One suffering *for* the guilty : but there was not, and could not be, One suffering the punish- ment *of* the guilty. All things come not alike to all ; for a man's inner spirit makes his own heaven or hell.

L

LECTURE XXIII.

Sunday Afternoon, March 2, 1851.

GENESIS xli.

THE history of Joseph in Egypt is interesting and valuable, not merely as a narrative of events, but for deeper reasons. This book of Genesis was written by Moses in reference to the peculiar characteristics of the people he was about to emancipate. He told them of the creation of the world, in order to teach them that the God whom he was telling them of was the God, not only of their land, but of the whole universe. He taught them respecting the original sabbath rest of God to explain to them the institution of their own sabbath. He told them of the original character of their forefathers, to show them that it was no new worship to which he was going to lead them. And in telling them this history of Joseph, one reason for it manifestly was to give them a reason for their being in Egypt, and to raise their spirit by telling them that originally they were princes in the land and not slaves as they then were. Again, these Jewish histories are remarkable for the religious, pious character of those of whom they treat. Every nation venerates its forefathers; but the peculiarity of those of the Jews was that they were not merchant princes or conquerors but pious saints of God, the central principle of their life being faith.

The subject of this chapter will divide itself into these two branches.

I. The summoning of Joseph to interpret Pharaoh's dream.

II. The interpretation of that dream.

I. The summoning of Joseph to interpret Pharaoh's dream.

Observe here first of all the long waiting of Joseph before he attained his emancipation. For two long years he lingered in that prison; the best and wisest man in the land was shut up for two of the best years of his life. At first sight there seems something wrong here; but we soon see the wisdom of this delay. First, in respect to Joseph's character; for it was in this prison that he was learning lessons of the soul, God's lessons. When God teaches man a lesson, he perhaps will not be able to put it into words and keep it as a maxim of life; it is something that he cannot express, but only feel. Such a lesson was Joseph learning. How long did it take to make the young dreamer unlearn the spirit of censoriousness, of self complacency? Those two years, instead of being long, were short to learn such precious lessons in.

Again, we see the wisdom of this delay in respect of Joseph's circumstances. Had he been released before, he might have returned to his father's house or re-entered that of Potiphar; and then what would have become of the land of Egypt? The lesson to be drawn from this is a very simple one—that of trust and faith and patience. It will occur, in future life, to many here to be suspected as Joseph was, to have obloquy resting on their character. They are not to go forward to defend their character, but simply to wait. We are here we know scarcely for what—not to act

alone certainly, but to suffer and to learn; and what we have
to do is to bear patiently, to feel that all is right.

The next thing in this summoning of Joseph is Pharaoh's
prophetic dream. Such dreams and forewarnings occur not in
Scripture alone. It is impossible to deny that in certain cases
events distant in the future do become known, unless we are prepared to deny the testimony of all ages. This dream occurred,
not to a holy man, but to a heathen: therefore the power
of prophecy tells nothing of the religious character. Balaam
saw the vision of the Almighty as truly as did the holy Isaiah;
hence it is that we degrade the Jewish prophets when we look
on them simply as predicters. Generally speaking, they foretold
the future because they clearly understood the present. This
tells us the difference between spiritual gifts and graces; gifts
belong to the intellect, graces to the heart. The apostle Paul
postponed all gifts to graces. Thus he says, "Covet earnestly
the best gifts; yet show I unto you a more excellent way.
Though I speak with the tongues of men and angels, and
have not charity, I am nothing."

The last thing I observe here is the chief butler's forgetfulness. Now there is a morbid feeling which delights in railing
against human nature; but it seems to me that there is a wiser
lesson to be gained from this story than merely speaking of the
butler's ungratefulness. Consider, first, the suspense in which
he was respecting his trial, and then the onerous duties that he
had to perform. Then remember, too, that what Joseph did
for him after all was not so much, it was merely the interpretation of his dream. The lesson that we draw from this is : in
this world we do too little and we expect too much. We bless

a poor man by giving to him, and we expect that we have made him our debtor for life. You fancy that the world has forgotten you. Reason with yourselves. For this world, from which you expect so much, what have you done? And if you find that you have done little and received much, what marvel is it that you receive no more? The only marvel is, that we have received so much.

Respecting this forgetfulness, there is something else to learn. During those two years Joseph had been as a "dead man clean out of mind." At the end of that time he came to the remembrance of the butler. It is doubtful whether a thing can ever be quite taken from the mind; what is buried there will rise again. Hence it is that no guilty deed can simply be forgotten. Time is nothing to memory. You cannot cement the deed to the spot of performance; go where you will, it accompanies you! An awful, awful thought for each of us when we intend to commit a sin! But here a difficulty arises; if this be true, how can there be a heaven for us? certainly heaven cannot exist to us while burdened with the remembrance of sin. This very difficulty must have presented itself to the ancient Greeks. The remedy they imagined for it was this; that before the spirit entered the land of blessedness, it must pass through the waters of Lethe to produce oblivion. Here we have a mighty instinct of the soul. Christ came not to destroy it but to fulfil it. In Him we attain the power and the right to forget the past. So long as we remain unregenerated and unconverted, the past is ours; but, regenerated in Christ, there is a sense in which we have a right to forget the past. In the words of Scripture, we "put off the

old man, and put on the new, renewed in Christ." Christ i
our river of forgetfulness.

II. The interpretation of the dream.

Observe the graceful way in which Joseph refers all to God
He says, " It is not in me : God shall give Pharaoh an answe:
of peace." Observe also his calmness ; this was produced b
the consciousness of God's presence. He was not there t
consider what men would think of him ; he felt that the gif
was from God. It is only this feeling that can effectually
crush the flutterings of vanity. "What hast thou," says the
apostle, " that thou didst not receive ? "

Again, in the interpretation of the dream observe Joseph':
plan ; it was simply a prudential foresight for the future
This prudence is a Christian virtue ; but it is hardly neces
sary to bring this before you, so common is it in this land
of England. It is our bounden duty to show how far this
rises to the rank of a Christian virtue. It is a virtue only
so far as it has no reference to self. If we save in one thing
to spend on another, it may be a virtue, but certainly it is not
a Christian one ; that alone is Christian which is done for the
sake of others. Thus, if we retrench our expenses in order to
have more to bestow on others, it is Christian. Thus did
Joseph ; his economy was all for the sake of others.

Now, in conclusion, I have only one practical inference to
draw from this history, the same that was taught by our Master in the parable of the unjust steward. He commended
the unjust steward because he had done wisely ; he was wiser
in his generation than the children of light ; he had used his
opportunity. Our Redeemer tells us that where he gained we

fail; we have our advantages, and we, the children of light, neglect to use them for the future. The same lesson is taught by Joseph's history. To us, the years in which we are living are those of plenty, abundance of spiritual instruction; but the years of dearth will come. Blessed is the man who shall use the present well. Blessed is he who makes use of the present opportunity, who is using the present in acquiring spiritual strength. Blessed is he who is laying up for himself, while on earth, a treasure in the heavens which shall never fail.

LECTURE XXIV.

Sunday Afternoon, March 16, 1851.

GENESIS xlii.

IN this chapter we have two subjects to consider.
    I. Joseph's administration in the land of Egypt.
II. The first journey of his brethren thither to buy corn.
I. Joseph's administration in the land of Egypt.

Here we notice first of all those qualifications which Pharaoh recognised as fitting Joseph for the situation of governor. He said, "Can we find such a one as this is, a man in whom the Spirit of God is?" (chap. xli. 38.) The Bible speaks of inspiration in a much more extended sense than we do, it marks every gift as specially of God. Still we must remember that a spiritual gift does not necessarily make a spiritual man. Balaam, for instance, was gifted with the highest powers of poetry; he had, too, the power of seeing future events; and yet he dies a bad man, far from God. But Joseph was inspired in the highest and truest sense. Not only was he spiritually gifted to rule the nation, but he had also that higher gift which enabled him to refer the lower gift to God. Now there are three things required to fit a man to rule: intellectual power, a sense of dependence upon God, and unselfishness. All these were combined in Joseph; we are told that there "was none so discreet and wise as he." In the interpretation that he gave to Pharaoh's dreams we ee how he referred all to God; his unselfishness we see in is forgiveness of his brethren. Without these qualities there an be no real rule; for it is these which make up saintliness, nd saintliness alone fits a man to rule perfectly. But saintli- ness in the sense we use it must take in intellectual power for mere spiritual goodness alone does not make a good uler. Eli was a good man, he had the two latter qualities which go to make up a ruler; but he was wanting in the irst, he was a weak man, and this it was which caused such roubles to his country. But it is a mistake still greater to suppose that intellectual power alone qualifies for rule. There must also be moral goodness and unselfishness. These are the qualities which clarify the intellect and purify the character.

We next observe the naturalization of the Hebrews. Joseph was made governor over Egypt, and admitted to all the privi- leges of that exclusive nation; yet in the midst of this Joseph never forgot his own family, his country, his home, and, above all, his God. "By faith," we read, "he gave commandment concerning his bones," that they should rest in his own land. Now, what Canaan was to the Jew, that heaven is to the Christian. St. Paul says that our citizenship is to be in heaven. In this we may learn a lesson from the Israelites, for wherever the Jew was found, his desires were always on Canaaɪ, Zion, Jerusalem. We are strangers and pilgrims here; this is not our home. We are to be in the world, but not of the world; we are to drink of its pleasures, but not to allow them to intoxicate us. Our outward conversation is in the world, but our inward life, our citizenship, is to be hid with Christ in God.

II. The first journey of Joseph's brethren into Egypt.

We notice, first, the famine in Canaan, which had extended thither from the land of Egypt. Abraham, Isaac, and Jacob were all driven to Egypt by famine. The origin of moral evil must remain to us a mystery, but that of physical evil ought not to be so. To the philosopher and the speculative man it is a mystery, but not so in the cottage and on the sick bed. Where pain is really felt, there its meaning is understood. Spiritual good is utterly impossible without physical evil.

We next observe the office of conscience. " They said one to another, We are verily guilty concerning our brother," etc. (ver. 21.) Where sin is voluntary wrong doing, the language of the human heart inevitably connects the penalty with the wrong doing. Let us here collect something that may serve us as a guide through life. In every temptation that comes upon you, think what it will be in the hour of death to be free from the recollection of it. Refrain, refrain, remember the hereafter. In Reuben, remark, there is something that tells more of selfishness than of love ; and yet in a measure he was right in linking the penalty to the sin. When the cock crew, the Redeemer looked upon Peter, reminding him of his error without the utterance of a word.

Next, observe the severity in the love of Joseph ; this we have in the seventh verse : "he made himself strange unto his brethren, and spake roughly unto them." He did not allow his personal feelings to interfere with what seemed to him his duty. Joseph's love to his brethren was a noble love. God's love to us is still nobler, and severity accompanies it. It does not shrink from human suffering, for suffering is necessary for the man's well being.

Lastly, we remark on the return homewards of Joseph's brethren. Jacob expected corn to relieve their necessities; he got the corn, but with it came sorrow upon sorrow. Bereaved of Joseph, he is now bereaved of Simeon also. In Jacob's answers to his sons, in the close of the chapter, we find a depth of querulousness and despondency. Job was tried with sorrows far more severe, and yet they only served and contributed to the purifying of his spirit. In order to understand the cause of Jacob's despondency we must go far back. Jacob was a selfish man; his very religion was selfish; he would become religious only on condition that God would protect and guide him. To that selfish origin may be traced all the evils of his after life. Throughout it seems to have been his principle to receive as much as possible, and to give as little as he could. He who lives in this world for his own personal enjoyment, without God and His Christ, will by degrees find, like Jacob, that he has no rock to rest his soul upon, but that he must go down in sorrow to the grave.

LECTURE XXV.

Sunday Afternoon, March 23, 1851.

GENESIS xliii.

THE 43rd chapter contains the history of the second journey of Jacob's sons into the land of Egypt. Between the two journeys there was an interval of unknown duration. We only know that it lasted so long as the first supply of corn remained to them.

The history divides itself into these two branches:

I. The journey.

II. The arrival in Egypt.

I. The journey. Observe here:

1. The resolve of Jacob to send at last his son Benjamin to Egypt. When the proposal was first mentioned to him, he positively refused to part with the lad. Reuben had said, "Slay my two sons if I bring him not to thee: deliver him into my hand, and I will bring him to thee again" (chap. xlii. 37). An arrangement in which, although there was a dim shadow of the great principle of atonement, yet it was mixed up with the notions of bloodshed and revenge. But that proposal was at once rejected; now, however, we find Judah making another which is accepted: "I will be surety for him; of my hand shalt thou require him: if I bring him not unto thee, and set him before thee, then let me bear the blame for ever" (ver. 9). In this consent of Jacob

we read a double instance of faith, faith in God and in man. Faith in God; for he says, "God Almighty give you mercy before the man" (ver. 14). Faith has been well defined thus, "the heart to make ventures for God." He alone knows what real faith is, who has been compelled to lose sight of or to relinquish hold of those most dear to him, relying only on the mercy and eternal love of God. Faith is that which makes us hold and cling to God when nothing else is left for us to cling to ; the grasp of the dying sailor to the mast, that is faith. There was, besides, faith in humanity, in his son Judah, in one scarcely worthy of his confidence, for once at least he had proved treacherous. But it was better so, and it is better for us if we possess this faith in man. We must not always be suspecting those about us. Better far to be deceived once or twice in our lives than to be for ever suspecting that our servants and children are always on the watch to rob us.

2. Jacob's honesty. He commanded his sons to take back the money which had been returned in their sacks. "Peradventure," said he, "it was an oversight" (ver. 12). This is the strictness of religious honesty. We are bound not only to return that which is ours unjustly, but also that which is ours by the oversight or mistake of others.

But there is another way of looking at this act of Jacob's. It seems somewhat to savour of his disposition to mollify and appease his enemies by presents ; as, when he dreaded the enmity of Esau, he sent presents to him, flattering him with the name of god. And if it be so, we find here that which tells, not of honesty, but of pliancy. We have just the opposite to this in the case of Paul when brought before Felix. The Roman governor hoped that some reward would have been given him to release his prisoner. But no; Paul stood firm, resolved never to buy his liberty. A higher example still is given us in the trial of Christ. Pilate says, "Knowest Thou not that I have power to crucify Thee and have power to release Thee?" thereby indirectly asking for a bribe; but the Redeemer answered not a word that might indulge such a hope. But specially is this pliancy of character dangerous when it becomes the tone of mind towards God, when by the indulgence of this spirit of appeasing by presents there is gradually formed in us a false conception of God's character, and we begin to think that He may be bought, and bribed, and flattered.

3. The change of Jacob's resolution in permitting Benjamin to go. At first we might be inclined to charge him with inconsistency, but the circumstances were changed, and the only choice now left him was between famine for them all and the loss of one son. If a man is never to change his line of conduct, and is ever fearing that if he does so and so it will appear inconsistent with his former course, then manifestly conversion is impossible. The Christian man, who desires to live and be the truth, is not to be for ever endeavouring to make his present conduct coincide with the acts and thoughts that have gone before. He must be true to his present convictions, leaving the past to reconcile itself to the present as it may.

II. The arrival.

1. The first incident we notice here is the fear of Joseph's

brethren when invited to Joseph's house. They came dreading some misfortune. They were suspicious of Joseph's intentions. They could not but think that he wished to entrap them and make bondsmen of them. And this fear of theirs arose partly out of their own capability for a similar act of treachery. 'Thus conscience doth make cowards of us all." It is the worst penalty of a deceitful and crooked disposition that it always dreads being overreached.

2. In the next place we observe the bowing down of the brethren before Joseph (ver. 26). This was an exact fulfilment of one of his early dreams, when the sun, moon, and eleven stars bowed down before him. But Joseph was now changed; he had been too much saddened by misfortune, and was far too much accustomed to Egyptian homage, to find any real pleasure in this, from which he had formerly expected so much. For us this is a pregnant example of the illusiveness of human life. Now that his dream was fulfilled to the very letter, he could not enjoy it. That thing which he had seen before in the prophetic visions of youth, that thing he had got; and now the joy of it was not in that, in the superiority, but in quite other circumstances. So it is we live, looking to an horizon which we reach but cannot enjoy, in which we find not what we expected. And yet observe here the merciful arrangement of God, who thus leads us on. Could we now count the cost of the things we hope for, would it be possible to live?

3. We next observe Joseph's relief in the indirect utterance of his feelings. He asked, " Is your father yet alive, and your youngest brother?" etc. (ver. 27.) Here is a strange principle of our nature, the necessity of utterance, either by a direct or

by an indirect channel. Thus, criminal feeling must find for itself either direct expression in confession, or in speaking of the deed as committed by another.

4. We next remark the feast of brotherhood. When that paroxysm of joy was over which drew tears from Joseph's eyes, he appeared again, and commanded a feast to be set before them. That feast broke no difference of rank, for Joseph had a table to himself; neither did it interfere with Egyptian etiquette. The Hebrews and Egyptians were placed at different tables. Observe also, though a feast of brotherhood, it pretended to no equality. Joseph made no pretension of loving them all alike. So is it with Christian brotherhood; first, it does not break through ranks, but it enunciates a principle which by degrees will make all ranks equal. Secondly, it does not rudely break through any custom which does not trench on any principle of right. Lastly, it never falsely pretends that all are equal; it does not say that Benjamin, who has offended little and loved much, shall receive only the same as the others. It tells us that those most like to Christ shall be most dear to God. Likeness to Christ. resemblance to the life of Christ, and the intense and utter happiness that comes from that, that is the five-foldness of Benjamin.

LECTURE XXVI.

Sunday Afternoon, March 30, 1851.

GENESIS xliv.

THE chapter we have to expound to-day contains the well known account of the second departure of Joseph's brethren from Egypt, and their quick return to the palace. There is, however, one thing that we must first dispose of, and that is, the fact of the existence of a divining cup in Joseph's house. This shows us that Joseph had given way to Egyptian superstition; and therefore those commentators who desire to make Joseph appear blameless have endeavoured to give a meaning to this word "divining" which it will not bear. But we must remember that Joseph and the other saints of the Old Testament all belonged to ages before, and not after, Christ. They were before their generations, or they would not have been saints; but not before all generations, or they would have been more than saints. There are two divisions in the subject of this chapter.

I. The test to which Joseph exposed his brethren.

II. Their conduct under that test.

I. The test to which Joseph exposed his brethren.

There is at first sight an apparent wantonness in the manner in which this was applied; but looking deeper we see some motives for such a mode of action. Probably it was designed as a kind of penalty for their former deeds. Joseph had been

M

basely treated. Though he forgave his injurers, yet it was good
for them to see their crime and feel it. His was not mere
maudlin compassion ; he desired first to bring them to repentance, and then he was ready and willing to forgive. And
in this he is a type of God ; God is the infinitely Forgiving
One, but the Just One besides. When God forgives, let it
not be supposed that no penalty ensues. Oh that we could
fasten this truth upon our minds, that every sin brings with
it a penalty which still remains even though the sin be pardoned by the blood of Christ. David sins, and the merciful
Lord puts away his sin ; but still the beloved child must die.

And a second motive which may be assigned for
Joseph's conduct is that perhaps it was to compel them to
feel that their lives were in his power. They are humbled
to the dust before him by the test. Now, in assigning to
him such a natural motive, we are not showing his conduct
as anything superhuman. It was magnanimous, but yet mixed
with the human. Everything that man does has in it something of evil ; even his best actions have in them something
that will not bear the light of day.

Again Joseph may have wished to test his brethren's
capability of forgiveness. When Benjamin came not with
them at the first, Joseph perhaps doubted whether he had
not been disposed of, as he himself had been ; therefore did
he contrive that Benjamin should be brought before him.
But when this matter was set at rest, there was still another
question to be decided. How was he treated by the brothers?
This he tested by putting the cup into his sack. Had they
believed in their brother's guilt, and refused to pardon him

this would have proved that they themselves were unfit to receive pardon. This condition for receptivity of forgiveness is set forth by Christ when He tells us, " If ye forgive not men their trespasses, neither will your heavenly Father forgive you "; and this He illustrates by the parable of the unmerciful servant.

II. The conduct of Joseph's brethren under the test.

Judah was the spokesman; in his speech we observe the entire suppression of denial or excuse for Benjamin. They knew not what to think; they could not believe that he had really taken it, and yet the evidence was strong against him. Judah cannot prove that his brother is not guilty, neither can he believe that he is guilty; he therefore leaves that question entirely aside. Instead of denying it, in modern language he showed cause why the law should not be put in force against him.

We next notice the pathos of that speech. Read the 20th verse: " And we said unto my lord, We have a father, an old man, and a child of his old age, a little one ; and his brother is dead, and he alone is left of his mother, and his father loveth him." We ask, When will fiction produce pathos equal to that ? His appeal to Joseph was threefold; first, he appealed to his compassion; secondly, to his justice, for if Benjamin were guilty he had not forced himself into the temptation, but had been led into it by Joseph. He also appealed to Joseph's sense of that which is heroic and self devoted; for he offered to accept slavery in his brother's stead: " Now therefore I pray thee, let thy servant abide instead of the lad a bondman to my lord, and let the lad go up with his brethren." Had Benjamin been really guilty, and Joseph not his brother, he must have had a heart of flint to refuse the appeal of self devotion.

Let us learn, in conclusion, that even in the worst of mankind there is something good left. Judah was by no means an immaculate man; but from what a man was, you cannot be certain what he is now. Here were men virtually guilty of the sin of murder, really guilty of cupidity in selling their brother; but years after we find in them something tender still, love for their father and compassion for their brother. It is this spark of undestroyed good in man that the Spirit of Christ takes hold of; and he alone who is able to discover this in the hearts of the worst, he alone will be in this world successful in turning sinners to God.

LECTURE XXVII.

Sunday Afternoon, April 6, 1851.

GENESIS xlv.

THE conclusion of the last chapter gives us an account of the successful pleading of Judah for Benjamin. This intercession of Judah resembles in many respects that of our Lord for His people; not because it is a type in the common acceptation of the word, that is, a thing contrived beforehand to be the resemblance of a future thing; but it is a type on this principle, that as the intercession of our Lord is true and real, so it must partake of the principle of every other intercession that is true and real. There is a likeness between Judah's and Christ's intercession, first, in that the intercessor was related to him for whom he interceded; so is it with our Lord, He is our Elder Brother, we His brethren in the flesh. Secondly, Judah resembles Christ, because the temptation had been shared but not yielded to. The crime of which Benjamin appeared to be guilty had been as much brought before Judah, who withstood it. He had therefore those things which qualify a man for sympathy; and such was the complete fitness of our Redeeming Master. "He was in all points tempted like as we are, yet without sin." Tempted, sinless, therefore able in a twofold way to intercede for us; knowing what is due to God's offended law, and knowing what is also due to our frail human nature. Thirdly, there was likeness in this, in the self devotion

of brother for brother.   We are not to consider the sacrifice of
Christ as a solitary principle; it is a principle found throughout
life. So that in the self devotion of Judah we have that which
corroborates the sacrifice of Christ ; for if we deny the possibility of Judah's, we must also deny that of Christ.   Lastly,
there was a point of resemblance in this, that he who was to
pardon was already resolved to pardon.   Joseph was already on
the side of Benjamin.   The intercession was necessary for the
sake of proving Judah's love, but not for the sake of appeasing
Joseph's hatred.   And such is the principle of our Master's
sacrifice.   God already was on the side of man.   We err if we
suppose that that sublime and august sacrifice was to appease
the hatred of the Almighty ; it was the satisfaction of love, not
the appeasing of hatred ; thus we read, "God so loved the
world that He gave His only begotten Son," etc.

The exposition of this chapter divides itself into these two
branches :

I. Joseph's interview with his brethren.

II. Their summons by Pharaoh to dwell in the land of
Goshen.

I. The interview.

Observe the delicacy of Joseph's feelings in removing all
the witnesses of his emotion.   There are some persons who
rather love to have witnesses of their various feelings, and
feel no sense of shame when they have given utterance to
anything emotional before others.   By these means feelings
become vulgarized, weak, and frittered away.   That religious
feeling which is never at a loss for appropriate words is a religion and a sensibility which has in it no depth.   With deep

truth are we told this in the parable of the sower and the seed. He cast his seed on the stony ground, and the seed sprang up rapidly, simply because there was no depth of earth. Therefore from this we learn that feeling, to be true and deep, must be condensed by discipline. We are taught this by our Redeemer's life. The commonplace truths of life were given publicly; but those deeper ones were veiled in parables to the multitude and expounded alone to the disciples.

The second thing that we notice here is the entireness of Joseph's forgiveness. This may be inferred from his desire to prevent remorse. "Be not angry with yourselves," etc. (ver. 5–15.) And this fear of Joseph for his brethren was founded on reality, for there is a danger, a great danger, in remorse. When a man's or a woman's heart is absorbed in the thought of the painfulness of the past, nothing can be done in the present, penitence or true reformation of life becomes impossible. And a further proof of the entireness of Joseph's forgiveness is, that he referred the past to God's will (ver. 8). When a man speaks calmly, as Joseph did, you may rely upon it, the forgiveness is entire. Upon this we have three remarks to make. First, that it is utterly impossible for us to judge of any event, whether it is a blessing or misfortune, from simply looking at the event itself; because we do not know the whole. Fancy the buying of a slave in a cave in Canaan; and straightway there springs up in your breast a feeling of indignation. Pass on a few years, and we find Joseph happy, honoured, and beloved; two nations at least are saved by him from famine. Secondly, we remark how God educes good from evil, and that man is only an instrument in His hands. A secular historian, treating of mighty events, always infers that there has been some plan steadily pursued; he would have traced step by step how it all came about, and referred it all to Joseph. But from the inspired history we find that Joseph knew not one step before him. Thirdly, we remark that there is a danger in the too easy acquiescence in the fact that good comes from evil; for we begin to say, Evil then is God's agent, to do evil must be right; and so we are landed in confusion. Before this had taken place, had Joseph's brethren said, "Out of this, good will come, let us sell our brother," they would have been acting against their conscience; but after the event it was but faith to refer it to God's intention. Had they done this before, it would have been presumption. But to feel that good has come through you, but not by your will, is humiliating. You feel that the evil is all yours, and the good is God's.

II. The summons of Jacob by Pharaoh.

Remark, Pharaoh rejoiced with Joseph. It is common enough to hear complaints of man's ingratitude; but to an earnest mind the only wonder is, the superabundance of love he meets with. Love begets love. Joseph had been faithful, and Pharaoh honours and esteems him.

We here observe the advice given by Joseph to his brethren, "See that ye fall not out by the way." There was deep wisdom in this. On their return Reuben would probably have begun to taunt them and remind them how different would have been the result had they taken his advice; and each one separately would have found some cause of quarrel. We should do well to ponder on Joseph's advice, for when that wondrous message was given to the world that God had pardoned man, men at once began to quarrel with each other. They began to throw the blame on the Jew alone for having caused His death ; they began to quarrel respecting the terms of salvation.

Lastly, we remark the incredulity of Jacob, "his heart fainted." There are two kinds of unbelief, that which disbelieves because it hates the truth, and that which disbelieves because the truth is apparently too glorious to be received. The latter was the unbelief of Jacob; it may be an evidence of weakness, but not necessarily an evidence of badness. This was a similar case to Thomas ; he could not believe the words of those around him, he must see the outward manifestation before he could believe. It was a pitiable thing that Jacob should believe the evidence of the wagons more than the words of his sons, but it was human. From this we learn the real value of the outward evidences of Christianity ; they tell on impressible spirits : some could not believe without them. But far nobler was the faith of the centurion who could trust his God out of sight, that faith which can rest on God's existence and on His words without evidence.

LECTURE XXVIII.

Sunday Afternoon, May 4, 1851.

GENESIS xlviii. 15, 16.

THE portion of Scripture which lies before us for our exposition to-day consists of the 48th chapter of this book, together with the concluding verses of the 47th; the latter gives us the history of Joseph's administration in Egypt, and the former an account of the dying hour of Jacob; these then are our divisions for to-day.

Looking first at the administration of Joseph, we read that his foresight had filled the granaries with corn; to him therefore the people applied. From this time every man held his property and his life in fiefship to the king; everything became the property of the state. This suggests to us two parallel cases, the constitution of ancient Israel and of modern England. In ancient Israel we find something parallel. When the destroying angel passed over the houses of the Egyptians, slaying their firstborn, the firstborn of the Israelites were spared. It was then held that every Israelite was bought with blood, and the firstborn of every family offered sacrifice for himself. By degrees, as the history of the nation passed on, there was an enactment made which substituted for the firstborn of Israel one tribe, consecrated to be priests by the right ear and foot being touched with blood, signifying that it was the duty of the priest to do nothing but what was consecrated by the love of God. If we remember that the tribe of Levi represented the whole nation of Israel, we shall then understand the tenure upon which each man was in covenant with God; he was touched with blood, and thus every power of seeing, feeling, hearing, etc., was all consecrated to Jehovah's service.

We find also this principle in the constitution of England. The king is the supreme lord of all property; against the king every crime that is committed is considered to be done. Now this principle in three different nations rests in every case on a separate historical fact. In the case of Egypt it rested on the preserving the people from famine, in that of Israel in passing over the firstborn, and in that of England on the conquest of the country by one of its ancient kings. From which we learn that the principle is all we have to deal with; and we arrive at this conclusion, that that which Joseph meant to teach was the right of monarchy and the duty of the people to their king. In the case of Israel, that which was to be taught was that God was their sovereign, representing to them the majesty of the law. And our loyalty we give to the sovereigns, not because they are the representatives of the majority of the people, but because they are the chosen symbols of that which assuredly came from no people's will, the eternal law of God, the law of right and wrong.

We pass on now, secondly, to consider the circumstances which belong to Israel's dying hour. And first we observe that the two grandsons of Jacob were taken to be present at his death bed. "And one told Joseph, Behold thy father is sick; and he took with him his two sons, Manasseh and Ephraim.

And Israel strengthened himself and sat upon his bed." This is the nearest approach in the Bible to that which is commonly termed a death bed scene. There is no sadder phrase than that—" a death bed scene"; for a man, when he comes to die, has something different to do than mere acting; it is not then his business to show other people how a Christian can die, but to prepare himself to meet his God. It is sad also because the dying hour is often unsatisfactory, often far from triumph; in the book of Ecclesiastes we read, " How dieth the wise man, as the fool." For there is stupor, sadness, powerlessness; and spiritual darkness also frequently clouds the last moments of the pious man. This dying hour must however have made an impression on these young men. In death itself there is nothing naturally instructive; but in this death there was simplicity, they saw the sight of an old man gathered ripe unto his fathers and they would remember in their gaiety and strength what all life at last must come to. Consider too the effect that must have been produced on Joseph. There had been nothing, that we are aware of, with which he had to reproach himself in his conduct to his father; there was therefore no remorse mixed with his sorrow, he was spared the sharpest pang of all. How different must the feeling of the other brethren have been; they would remember that there lay one dying whom they had wronged, one whom they had deceived.

We observe in the second place the adoption of these two sons of Joseph by their grandfather. Jacob says, " Let my name be named on them " (ver. 16), by which he meant that they were not to remain Egyptians, though naturally they were such, their mother an Egyptian and their father ruler in the land. When a young man has what we call brilliant prospects before him we congratulate him; in the spirit of the Bible we should rather congratulate him when he is called early to do a work, to achieve something, on the side of God against that of the world.

We observe too how Jacob speaks of Rachel (ver. 7). At first sight there appears in this no connection with what is written before or after it; but looking more attentively at it, the matter is plain; the old man thinks of Rachel, he remembers that these were the sons of Rachel's son, and he implies that it was for her sake that he adopted them. If there is anything that tells of a stain upon a man's heart, it is when he is able to speak in a tone of contempt of those purest first affections which constituted the glory of his early manhood; but it was not so with Jacob. One of the most elevating things that a man can have is a loss that goes near home. Jacob was the better for this loss of his beloved Rachel; he thence became less selfish than before; accordingly, when he came to Egypt, there was no unseemly rejoicing, as there would otherwise have been, over the brilliant prospects of his race; and the latter part of his life was that of affection rather than as formerly of avarice. Lastly on this subject, there is something in this long continuance of affection for the lost wife that seems to tell us something of the possibility of reunion. Upon this subject Scripture tells us almost nothing. When we look at the analogy of this world, and mark the growth of our affections as they develop in our life first to parents, then to brother, and then to wife, and then to child, each in some measure supplanting the other, we might be inclined to believe that there would be a perpetual growth of attachment to spirits higher and higher still; but when we see a feeling like this of Jacob, we cannot but hope that that which had lasted so near to the grave might survive the grave. We know not, God grant that it may!

Again, observe the eyes of Jacob were now dim. "Now the eyes of Israel were dim for age, so that he could not see" (ver. 10). Perhaps this might remind him of his conduct to his old blind father Isaac. In him we see all the powers of life fading, and we are tempted to say, Can this live for ever? The eye cannot see God, therefore the eye fails; the ear cannot hear Him, therefore is it filled with dust; but faith and love, the things that are to survive the grave, exist in their strength up to the grave.

The last thing we notice is the consolation given to survivors. Jacob says, "Behold, I die, but God shall be with you," etc. (ver. 21). Thus our Redeemer said to His disciples, "It is expedient for you that I go away," etc. This then explains to us the principle of bereavement; slowly and by degrees all drops off from us—first our parents, then our companions, till at last we find ourselves alone, with no arm of flesh to support us; and then comes the sense of dependence on the arm Divine: therefore is it emphatically written that He is the God of the fatherless and the widow.

LECTURE XXIX.

Sunday Afternoon, May 11, 1851.

GENESIS xlix.

THIS chapter contains Jacob's predictions of the destinies of his descendants. The predictions are partly explicable on natural grounds. Jacob's sagacity was sufficient to distinguish the germs of character already shown in his sons, and from thence he could foretell the results. Reuben's instability for instance was the result of a sensual character. The nomad, fierce life of the Simeonites and Levites was the natural consequence of a cruel disposition.

But there is a part of this remarkable chapter which we cannot so get over: the prediction of Zebulon's future locality by the seaside; of the descent of the Saviour from Judah: events both of which took place after the settlement in Canaan. Here we are plainly out of the region of things cognizable by sagacity, and have got into the sphere of the prophetic faculty.

Observe that five of these sons have their fortunes specifically told, and in detail; the rest generally. We divide the chapter therefore into these two divisions.

I. The five specific prophecies.

II. The general history.

1. The first of the specific prophecies is that respecting Reuben, and is in two divisions: (1) an enumeration of his original circumstantial advantages, contrasted (2) with the destiny determined for himself by character.

(1) On the original advantages Jacob dwells minutely: "Reuben, thou art my firstborn, my might, and the beginning of my strength, the excellency of dignity, and the excellency of power" (ver. 3). He lingers on his natural advantages as if to say, "Compare what thou art with what thou mightest have been!" And it is full of bitter feeling to remember early hopes and expectations formed of us, to think what we are, and what we have not done! And the lesson is, that it is not privileges, but the use of privileges, that decides destiny. Your fate is put by God into your own hands.

(2) Contrasted with this, which Reuben might have been, is brought out sharply what he had made himself. "Unstable as water thou shalt not excel" (ver. 4). In the Epistle of St. James we find a double minded man described in a similar way, and a better illustration could not be ; for what is more unstable than water, yielding, tempestuous, treacherous, fierce, and feeble.

Observe this instability of Reuben's is traced to his life of sensuality. Apparently there is no connection between the two things, really there is the most close and intimate connection. He who cannot command his passions has no influence over others ; for the secret of rule is that a man should be able to rule himself. Only once do we hear of Reuben giving advice; it was when he stood alone, and recommended his brethren to spare Joseph, and then his advice was only partially taken. Such a man also is unable to excel in anything ; for, of course, a mind tossed with passion and desire is incapable of that steady perseverance to which success is given. We see this characteristic in the entrance into Canaan. The

Reubenites ask for the land east of Jordan; they cannot wait; they show the very characteristic of the man of sense who always places the present above the future, the seen above the unseen. They have not even ambition; low and mean are their tastes. Israel's honour and the glory of Israel's arms are nothing to them. They want to enjoy now, and prefer the gratifications of sense to those which charm nobler minds.

Compare again their conduct in Sisera's invasion. After Israel's victory a heroic war song was chanted by Deborah. It contains the account of the part which each of the tribes took in the war (Jud. v. 15, 16). The tribe of Reuben went not to the battle. Thus says Deborah: "Why abodest thou among the sheepfolds: to hear the bleatings of the flocks? for the divisions of Reuben there were great searchings of heart." Reuben, as usual, was enjoying himself, instead of fired with public spirit.

Learn therefore: First, Self rule is the condition of influence and success. Rule thyself, thou rulest all. To subject appetites is not a very high achievement; but for him who has not attained that first, simplest step in Christian life, excellence is impossible.

Next, learn how sin adheres to character. Years had passed since Reuben sinned. Probably he had forgotten what he had done. It was but a single act. But the act was not fixed to the spot which witnessed its performance. It went inwards, and made him irresolute, feeble, wretched, unstable. So with every sin, whether one of weakness or of violence. You are the exact result of all your past sins. There they are in your character. There is not a nerve in your body which

N

is not different in consequence of the sin from what it would
have been had the sin not been committed. And there is not
a feeling nor a thought which is not at this moment marked
and modified by your guilt. So the past must be for ever
present with us.

2, 3. The second and third of whom Jacob uttered his
predictions were Simeon and Levi. They were charged with
immoderate revenge. Observe, not revenge alone. "Cursed
be their anger, *for it was cruel*" (ver. 7). Had they not felt
anger, had they not avenged, they had not been men. That
responsibility which is now shared between judge, jury, the
law, and the executioner, was necessarily in early ages sustained
alone by the avenger of blood. That instinct of indignation
which is now regularly expressed by law was then of necessity
expressed irregularly. I do not think they were to be blamed
for doing the avenger's justice. But they slew a whole tribe.
The sin committed by one man was avenged on the whole
nation; they let their fury fall on the innocent cattle, for that
expression "they digged down a wall" is given thus in the
margin, "they houghed oxen," and nearly all commentators
are agreed that this is the true translation. The meaning
is that they cut the sinews of the brute beasts. Not satisfied
with wreaking their vengeance on man, they extended it
to the unoffending beasts. Now the penalty which fell on
them was of a very peculiar kind. It was said of them, " I
will divide them in Jacob and scatter them in Israel." This
has a plain meaning in Simeon's case, for his tribe was weak,
his territory divided: naturally so; for of course a ferocious wild
tribe would be like Arabs, scattered and unsettled. But in

Levi's case the prediction is not so intelligible as a penalty.
For Levi, though scattered in Israel, having no territorial
allotment, was a peculiarly privileged tribe; they were chosen
to be the tribe of priests. We consider this therefore as
one of the many, many cases in which a penalty is by grace
transmuted into a blessing. So too the curse of labour, now
the condition of mental and moral health; the subjection of
woman, made by meekness the school of heavenly humility.

4. Predictions respecting Judah. Of him four things are
said. First, his brethren should praise him: "Thou art
he whom thy brethren shall praise" (ver. 8). There is here,
so to speak, a play upon the word, for Judah signifies praise.
Observe, the blessing which legitimately belonged to one
of his three elder brothers had fallen on the fourth. We
should have expected him to be envied rather than praised
by them. But there is a spirit which can disarm envy. It
is that meekness which hides its own superiority, seems
unconscious of it, and even shows that it feels more pain
in surpassing than others can feel in being surpassed. Such
persons may be superior and still praised. A rare and
honourable peculiarity. "The meek shall inherit the earth."
Earth's inheritance, its praise and its love, belongs to such.

Next, Judah is put forward as the type of the Hebrew hero.
He is represented under the similitude of a lion. "He stooped
down, he couched as a lion, and as an old lion; who shall
rouse him up?" (ver. 9.) It has been remarked, perhaps not
idly, that the simile is a lion couchant, not rampant. Not the
strength of the oppressor, but that of one strong in right, the
majesty of defence: "who shall rouse him up?" And, indeed,

Judah's own character corresponds with this. Remember his self devotion in Benjamin's behalf (chap. xliv. 33). It is thus only that courage is redeemed from the mere brute qualities which are common to the lion as well as to man, and ranked with virtues properly Christian. Love and self devotion redeem instincts.

The third thing said respecting Judah brings us to the most difficult passage in Scripture: "The sceptre shall not depart," etc. (ver. 10.) Of the many interpretations that have been given of this only two are worth mentioning. According to the first the passage is to be read thus: "The sceptre shall not depart from Judah until he come to Shiloh, and the gathering shall be to him there;" *i.e.*, Judah's superiority over the other tribes shall continue until he come to Shiloh, "and to it the gathering of the tribes be." To understand this, see Judges xviii. 10, where the final settlement of the tribes is made at Shiloh; the review and the measurement; where the ark rested; and where, long afterwards, we find it (1 Sam. i.) while solemn sacrifices and yearly festivals are celebrated there. The interpretation then runs thus. So long as Israel shall assemble at Shiloh, and the tribes be gathered there, so long shall Judah be superior to his brethren: a poetical way of saying, for ages. The second interpretation is that commonly admitted among Christians, according to which Shiloh is a name for the Redeemer: Shiloh, the Pacificator, or Prince of Peace. Much has been written to evade the difficulty which arises from the fact that there was no king in Israel when He came. But surely it is not needed. Ten tribes disappeared. Of the remaining two, both merged themselves in Judah; and the sceptre is only a figurative and poetical name for nationality. Israel's nationality, merged in Judah, lasted until Shiloh came. We are brought therefore to this conclusion, that this is one of the first and clearest prophecies of a Redeemer.

Apparently there is a contradiction between the term Shiloh here used and the former metaphor of the lion. But a similar contrast occurs, with great beauty, in Revelation v. 5, 6 : " Weep not : behold, the Lion of the tribe of Judah hath prevailed . . , to open the book." Then comes the introduction of the seer into His presence : " And I beheld, and lo !"—a lion ? No—" a Lamb, as it had been slain." So that the two harmoniously declare a truth. There is a strength of force ; and there is another strength, the might and majesty of gentleness which is invincible through suffering, the glory of Him who is the Lion and the slain Lamb, the Lion *because* the Lamb.

The fourth prediction respecting Judah has reference to his temporal prosperity. His was to be a territory rich in vineyards and pastures (ver. 11, 12). " Binding his foal unto the vine and his ass's colt unto the choice vine ; he washed his garments in wine and his clothes in the blood of grapes ; his eyes shall be red with wine, and his teeth white with milk." It has been said that prosperity is the blessing of the Old Testament, tribulation the specific promise of the New. But this is scarcely true ; in the New, as in the Old, temporal blessings follow certain qualities of heart. The laws of God remain unalterable. The fifth commandment, " with promise," is quoted by Paul as valid in the Christian dispensation still. And in the

sermon on the mount Christ says : " Blessed are the meek !
for they shall inherit the earth."   The fact is not that the
consequences of right and wrong are changed, but that the
New Testament has brought out, with peculiar prominence,
a class of results of right doing which were only dimly visible
in the elder dispensation : the vision of God which belongs
to the pure in heart, the force which belongs to self control,
and others.   And these have thrown into shadow the earthly
advantages of well doing, as the sun makes the stars invisible.

5. We now come to Joseph, the last of those five of whom we
have a special prediction.   Here the whole tone of Jacob's
language changes.   It is, in fact, no longer prediction which
he utters, but an exuberant description of what Joseph was
and had been.   Take away the full and glowing prophecy of
general earthly happiness, and it is the natural result of such
a character.   The future is judged from the past.   When he
comes to Joseph the father's whole heart overflows.   Read
the whole, and you will see how the language swells into
fulness.   He is first a vine.   Then one who had been shot
at, injured, hurt, but escaped with strength.   Then comes a
burst of love and blessing.

Specially observe two things :—

(1.) An illustration in this blessing of the fulfilment and principle of the promise of the fifth commandment.   Joseph's
peculiarity was filial obedience ; and his lot above his brethren
was distinguished by worldly success and honour.   He was the
best governor Egypt had ever had.   The two were, however,
connected.   In childish obedience he learned fitness for rule.
He who can obey well is the only one who can well command.

Self reverence, self knowledge, self control—these three alone fit a man to be a ruler.

(2.) He had been "separate from his brethren" (ver. 26), and doubtless it was better for him, though an apparent disadvantage. Education and admixture with equals are two good things; but sometimes the deprivation of these things is better. He who is brought up like others often remains as others, whereas there is an individuality of character in which the angles have not been worn off, an originality, a difference from other men which is learned when we are separated from our brethren in stillness and solitude, in self education and lonely struggle.

II. General blessings on the seven remaining sons.

Probably the characteristic difference between these characters so given was recognised then, though lost to us now ; just as the difference between an inhabitant of Cumberland and one of Sussex is clear to us contemporaries, but in a few centuries will have disappeared. Verse 13 : Zebulun, a maritime power; Issachar, an agricultural tribe, remarkable for industry, peace (ver. 14, 15). Dan, remarkable for political sagacity (ver. 16, 17). Gad, a border tribe, exposed to danger, conquering danger by perseverance (ver. 19). Naphtali, gifted with eloquence (ver. 21). Asher, remarkable for plenty (ver. 20) and Benjamin for strength (ver. 27).

Now observe in all these different characters the true principle of unity. They are not lost in one undistinguished similarity, but each has its own peculiar characteristic : one made up of seamen ; another of shepherds ; one warlike, another cultivated ; and so on. And yet, together, one.

Their twelve loaves of shewbread remained for ever before the Lord on the altar, proclaiming their separateness, their characteristic differences, and their unity in working out one great purpose ; one in God by difference.

Apply this to Christian unity, and show how, by differences between man and man, church and church, nation and nation, the true organic unity is attained and kept.

Finally we have on all this chapter four reflections to make.

1. Jacob's spiritual character, as tested by his ejaculation, " I have waited for Thy salvation, O Lord" (ver. 18). A *religious* ejaculation from the dying patriarch breathless and exhausted with speech. Our exact character is tested by our spontaneous thoughts. Watch how the mind turns when pressure and coercion are taken off, and you know of what kind it is. Thus sudden events, sudden pangs, accidents, etc., determine for us the state of our souls, and show us the high-water mark of our spiritual attainment. From one man they wring a curse ; from another, a slang expression ; from a third, a natural prayer. Judge yourselves by this test. It would be dangerous to judge others always. But take it as a fair test of Jacob's state.

2. See what is assumed in this *personification* of the tribes. Judah, Simeon, Levi, are taken as the type of the future career of their several tribes. Every man impresses his character on his descendants. Those of marked character, of course, in a marked and perceptible way, so that in reading Ishmael's history, " a wild man," etc., you have the picture of every Arab to the present day. In Abraham's peculiarity,—a

man of faith—you have the peculiar history of Israel, a nation, not of soldiers, nor statesmen, but of saints. But that which is markedly true of each is true in a degree of all. The sin you commit to-day will surely tell upon the structure, constitution, and consequently moral state of all that shall rise out of your stock and lineage to the end of time. Let us add that to the innumerable motives for abstinence from sin.

3. Think of this father's feelings as his family gathered round him. Over each of those children a mother's heart had bled and a father's heart rejoiced. Their very names contained the record of such feelings: "Reu-ben"—lo! a son. Yes; and, lo! there he is; and what has he become? Happy is it for Christian fathers now, that in looking round on their assembled children they cannot read the future as Jacob did, that they are not able to fix on each of their sons and say, This for God and that for sin.

4. Lastly let us see here something that tells of the character of future judgment. Have you ever attended the opening of a will, where the bequests were large and unknown, and seen the bitter disappointment and the suppressed anger? Well; conceive those sons listening to the unerring doom. Conceive Reuben, or Simeon, or Levi listening to their father's words. Yet the day will come when, on principles precisely similar, our doom must be pronounced. Destiny is fixed by character, and character is determined by separate acts. The sensual life, and the passionate life, and the indolent life, each carries with it its own eternity, by a law contained in our own constitution, unalterably: "He that is filthy, let him be filthy still; and he that is holy let him be holy still." Brethren,

character determines eternity, acts determine character, and acts are determined by what we are. Now, not next week; now, not to-morrow; for to-morrow may lead you to a grave. Now let us turn unto the Lord and live, for now is the accepted time, now the day of salvation.

LECTURE XXX.

Sunday Afternoon, May 18, 1851.

GENESIS l. 12, 13.

THE commencement of the 49th chapter contains the history of Jacob's predictions of the destinies of his descendants. Very different was their lot; but there was one thing common among them, that their destiny was not according to original privilege, but to real character. It is not because we are born Christians that we are members of the eternal church of Christ. In God's world there are no favourites of heaven; all is decided by character.

Now we divide the subject of this discourse into two branches: first, the circumstances which preceded the death of Jacob; and afterwards, those which followed that death. Going back to the conclusion of the last chapter, we find that all his sons were personally blessed. In the 28th verse we read, "every one according to his blessing he blessed them." This might at first surprise us, for many of their privileges had been forfeited. However there is given us here a great truth the meaning of which becomes plain only by the gospel, and which permits us to make this distinction between the penalty that falls upon the sin (which is eternal) and that on the person (which may not be eternal). Sin must be put down: if you link yourself with sin, you too must be put down; and if you continue in sin, you must be crushed eternally with it. But in the mercy of God the gospel of Christ makes a distinction between the person and the sin.   There is in every one of us two men, the Adam and the Christ.   The Christian flees from sin, renounces it, will not acknowledge that it is part of himself; he detests, abhors it; he says, I fly from sin, help me against myself;

> " Rock of Ages, cleft for me,
>   Let me hide myself in Thee."

And he is forgiven.

We notice, secondly, Jacob's own conception of what death is.   He says, "I am to be gathered to my fathers" (ver. 29). Observe here the human associations that gather round his idea of death.   He fills the world beyond with his own race.   We do the same.   We people the world to come with those we have loved; without this we cannot form any conception of the future world.   In the parable of the rich man and Lazarus we read that Lazarus was seen in Abraham's bosom.   We might have thought it a more spiritual conception to have represented him as floating in the Eternal Light of God; but the Redeemer teaches not so.   It is an unreal state of mind which is fostered when we teach that spirituality is gained by a yearning for the world to come.   While this world contains those we love, to yearn after immortality is not spirituality but dissatisfaction and almost rebellion.   We desire to change those duties which are ours for those which are not ours.   Is that submission?   Shall we say that we are grateful to our Heavenly Father when we despise and spurn the things He has given us here to love?   But when the home here has been transplanted there, when in the world to come there are those whom we have lost, then to long to change this world for another is spiritual, because natural. God has given us the hope of another world, not to be continually hankering after it, but rather to be a support and stay in trouble, as Jacob here found it. Thus, every loss becomes God's gracious means of transplanting our affections from here to there.

We pass on now to consider Jacob's death, and the circumstances which followed it. The way in which he prepared for death is thus described, " he gathered his feet into the bed " (ver. 33), in other words, he prepared for death. He met death, he was not overtaken by it. It was not as if death had said to him, "Thou shalt come"; but as if he had said to death, "I will come." It is the unwilling necessity of death that makes it so terrible. I speak not now of the sting of death, but merely of the act of dying. The readiness to meet it which faith in Christ bestows is alone able to disarm it of its fearfulness. Thus, with the jailer at Philippi, he was ready and willing to die, so long as it seemed in his own power ; but as soon as the earth quaked, and he felt he had in it no power, he cried out as a very coward, " What must I do to be saved ? "

We next observe the mourning that followed Jacob's death, and this leads us to the 50th chapter. It was twofold, public and private. We are in the first verse told in touching language of the grief of Joseph: "and Joseph fell upon his father's face, and wept upon him, and kissed him." He had brought his children and listened calmly to his father's words; but when the last spark of life was gone his feelings gave way, and he wept. We next observe the public mourning, the description of which is given in the ninth and tenth verses : " and there went up with him both chariots and horsemen; and it was a very great company. And they came to the threshingfloor of Atad, which is beyond Jordan, and there they mourned." There are those who, in a utilitarian spirit, tell us that all this was a waste of time and of labour. In reply to which we say that these things, if they be a waste of time and wealth, at least do something of which utilitarianism takes no thought. Look, for example, at the mourning; what did it? It produced faith, it strengthened feeling, it gave time for the hearts of men to pause from this busy world of life and think of the world to come; and unless this inner life be going on, national wealth is but a mockery.

Jacob was embalmed, according to the custom of Egypt. This was done to retard the progress of corruption; for so long as the body was there, their friend seemed still among them. In that we find an intimation of immortality.

There now remains only one subject in the book for our consideration—the last forgiveness of Joseph to his brethren, which we reserve for a morning sermon rather than an afternoon exposition. At the close of a lecture it is impossible to give a review of the whole book; I therefore reserve it until next Sunday, when, by God's blessing, I shall hope to bring it before you.

LECTURE XXXI.

(PREACHED ON THE FIRST DAY OF PUBLIC MOURNING FOR
THE QUEEN DOWAGER, 1849.)

THE ISRAELITE'S GRAVE IN A FOREIGN
LAND.*

" And Joseph said unto his brethren, I die : and God will surely visit
you, and bring you out of this land unto the land which He sware to Abraham, to Isaac, and to Jacob.   And Joseph took an oath of the children of
Israel, saying, God will surely visit you, and ye shall carry up my bones
from hence.   So Joseph died, being an hundred and ten years old : and
they embalmed him, and he was put in a coffin in Egypt."—GENESIS
l. 24—26.

THERE is a moment when a man's life is re-lived on earth.
It is in that hour in which the coffin lid is shut down,
just before the funeral, when earth has seen the last of him for
ever.   Then the whole life is, as it were, lived over again in

---

* *This Sermon was formerly published by the Author in a separate form,
and the following Preface to that publication explains so well the circumstances under which all the other Sermons have been preserved, that it has
been thought best to reprint the Preface here.*

" For the publication of the commonplace observations contained in the
following pages, the commonplace excuse may perhaps suffice, that
printing was the simplest way of multiplying copies for a few friends who
desired them.   Perhaps too the uncommonness of the occasion may justify
the writer in giving to an ephemeral discourse an existence somewhat less
transient than the minutes spent in listening to it.

" The sermon is published as nearly as possible as it was spoken.   It
was written out concisely for a friend on the day of its delivery, with no
intention of publication.   Afterwards, it seemed better to leave it in that

the conversation which turns upon the memory of the departed. The history of threescore years and ten is soon recapitulated : not, of course, the innumerable incidents and acts which they contained, but the central governing principle of the whole. Feverish curiosity sometimes spends itself upon the last hours ; and a few correct sentences, implying faith after the orthodox phraseology, would convey to some greater hope than a whole life breathing the Spirit of Christ, separate from such sentences. But it is not thus the Bible speaks. It tells us very little of the closing scene, but a great deal of the general tenor of a life. In truth, the closing scene is worth very little. The felon who, up to the last fortnight, has shown his impenitence by the plea of not guilty, in the short compass of that fortnight makes a confession, as a matter of course exhibits the externals of penitence, and receives the Last Supper. But it would be credulity, indeed, to be easily persuaded that the eternal state of such a one is affected by it. A life of holiness sometimes mysteriously terminates in darkness ; but it is not the bitterest cries of forsakenness, so often the result of physical exhaustion, nor even blank despair, that shall shake our deep convic-

---

state, with only a few corrections, and the addition of a few sentences, than to attempt to re-write it after an interval too great to recall what had been said. This will account for the abruptness and want of finish which pervades the composition.

"The writer takes this opportunity of disowning certain sermons which have been published in his name. They would not have been worth notice, had not the innumerable blunders of thought and expression which they contain been read and accepted by several as his. For this reason he feels it due to himself to state that they are published without his sanction, and against his request, and that he is not responsible for either the language or the ideas."

tion that he whose faith shone brightly through life is now safe in the Everlasting arms. The dying scene is worth little, little at least to us, except so far as it is in harmony with the rest of life.

It is for this reason that the public estimate pronounced upon the departed is generally a fair criterion of worth. There are, of course, exceptional cases: cases in which the sphere of action has been too limited for the fair development of the character, and nothing but the light of the judgment day can reveal it in its true aspect; cases in which party spirit has defaced a name, and years are wanted to wash away the mask of false colour which has concealed the genuine features; cases in which the champion of truth expires amidst the execrations of his contemporaries, and after ages build his sepulchre. These, however, are exceptions. For the most part, when all is over, general opinion is not far from truth. Misrepresentation and envy have no provocatives left them. What the departed was is tolerably well known in the circle in which he moved. The epitaph may be falsified by the partiality of relations; but the broad judgment of society reverses that, rectifies it, and pronounces with perhaps a rude, but on the whole fair, approximation to the truth.

These remarks apply to the history of the man whose final scene is recorded in the text. The verdict of the Egyptian world was worth much. Joseph had gone to Egypt, some years before, a foreigner; had lived there in obscurity; had been exposed to calumny; by his quiet, consistent goodness, had risen, step by step, first to respect, then to trust, command, and veneration; was embalmed after death in the affections, as well as with the burial rites, of the Egyptians; and his honoured form reposed at last amidst the burial place of the Pharaohs.

In this respect the text branches into a twofold division. The life of Joseph; and the death which was in accordance with that life.

1. The history of Joseph, as of every man, has two sides: its outward circumstances and its inner life.

The outward circumstances were chequered with misfortune. Severed from his home in very early years, sold into slavery, cast into prison, at first grief seemed to have marked him for her own. And this is human life. Part of its lot is misery. There are two inadequate ways of accounting for this mystery of sorrow. One, originating in a zeal for God's justice, represents it as invariably the chastisement of sin, or at the least as correction for fault. But, plainly, it is not always such. Joseph's griefs were the consequences, not of fault, but of rectitude. The integrity which, on some unknown occasion, made it his duty to carry his brethren's "evil report" to their father, was the occasion of his slavery. The purity of his life was the cause of his imprisonment. Fault is only a part of the history of this great matter of sorrow. Another theory, created by zeal for God's love, represents sorrow as the exception, and happiness as the rule of life. We are made for enjoyment, it is said, and on the whole there is more enjoyment than wretchedness. The common idea of love being that which identifies it with a simple wish to confer happiness, no wonder that a feeble attempt is made to vindicate God, by a reduction of the apparent amount of pain.

Unquestionably however, love is very different from a desire to shield from pain. Eternal love gives to painlessness a very subordinate place in comparison of excellence of character. It does not hesitate to secure man's spiritual dignity at the expense of the sacrifice of his well being.

The solution will not do. Let us look the truth in the face. You cannot hide it from yourself. " Man is born to sorrow as the sparks fly upwards." Sorrow is not an accident, occurring now and then ; it is the very woof which is woven into the warp of life. God has created the nerves to agonize, and the heart to bleed ; and before a man dies, almost every nerve has thrilled with pain, and every affection has been wounded. The account of life which represents it as probation is inadequate : so is that which regards it chiefly as a system of rewards and punishments. The truest account of this mysterious existence seems to be that it is intended for the development of the soul's life, for which sorrow is indispensable. Every son of man who would attain the true end of his being must be baptized with fire. It is the law of our humanity, as that of Christ, that we must be perfected through suffering. And he who has not discerned the Divine Sacredness of Sorrow, and the profound meaning which is concealed in pain, has yet to learn what life is. The Cross, manifested as the Necessity of the Highest Life, alone interprets it.

2. Besides this, obloquy was part of Joseph's portion. His brethren, even his father, counted him a vain dreamer, full of proud imaginings. He languished long in a dungeon with a stain upon his character. He was subjected to almost all the bitterness which changes the milk of kindly feelings into gall :

to Potiphar's fickleness, to slander, to fraternal envy, to the ingratitude of friendship in the neglect of the chief butler who left his prison and straightway forgot his benefactor. Out of all which a simple lesson arises, " Cease ye from man, whose breath is in his nostrils." Yet that may be over-stated. Nothing chills the heart like universal distrust. Nothing freezes the genial current of the soul so much as doubts of human nature. Human goodness is no dream. Surely we have met unselfishness, and love, and honour among men. Surely we have seen, and not in dreams, pure benevolence beaming from human countenances. Surely we have met with integrity that the world's wealth could not bribe, and attachment which might bear the test of any sacrifice. It is not so much the depravity as the frailty of men, that makes it impossible to count on them. Was it not excusable in Jacob, and even natural, if he attributed to vanity his son's relation of the dream in which the sun, and the moon, and the eleven stars, bowed down before him? Was it not excusable if Potiphar distrusted his tried servant's word, when his guilt appeared so indisputably substantiated? Was not even the chief butler's forgetfulness intelligible, when you remember his absorbing interest in his own danger and the multiplied duties of his office? The world is not to be too severely blamed, if it misrepresents us. It is hard to reach the truth, very hard to sift a slander.

Men who believe such rumours, especially in courtly life, may be ignorant, hasty, imperfect, but are not necessarily treacherous. Yet, even while you keep this in mind, that the heart may not be soured, remember your dearest friend may fail you in the crisis; a truth of experience was wrapped up in the old fable, and the thing you have fostered in your bosom may wound you to the quick; the one you have trusted may become your accuser, and throw his own blame with dastard meanness upon you. That was the experience of Joseph. Was not that HIS fate who trusted Judas? There is One, and but One, whose Love is as a rock, which will not fail you when you cling. It is a fearful, solitary feeling, that lonely truth of life; yet not without a certain strength and grandeur in it. The life that is the deepest and the truest will feel most vividly both its desolation and its majesty. We live and die alone. God and our own souls—we fall back upon them at last. "Behold, the hour cometh, yea is now come, that ye shall be scattered, every man to his own, and shall leave Me alone; and yet I am not alone, because the Father is with Me."

3. Success, besides, marked the career of Joseph. Let us not take half views of men and things. The woof of life is dark; that we granted: but it is shot through a web of brightness. Accordingly, in Joseph's case, even in his worst days, you find a kind of balance, to be weighed against his sorrows. The doctrine of compensation is found through all. Amidst the schemings of his brothers' envy he had his father's love. In his slavery he had some recompence in feeling that he was gradually winning his master's confidence. In his dungeon he possessed the consciousness of innocence, and the grateful respect of his fellow prisoners.

In that beautiful hymn which some of you read last Sunday,*

---

* Keble's "Christian Year:" Twenty-fifth Sunday after Trinity.

you may remember that a parallel is drawn between human life and the aspects of the weather. The morning rainbow, glittering among the dangerous vapours of the west, predicts that the day will not unclouded pass away. The evening rainbow declares that the storms are past, and that serene weather is setting in. Such is the life of all whom God disciplines. The morning or the evening brightness is the portion of a life, the rest of which is storm. Rarely are the manful struggles of principle in the first years of life suffered to be in vain. Joseph saw the early clouds which darkened the morning of his existence pass away; and the rainbow of heavenly peace arched over the calmness of his later years. "The Lord was with Joseph, and he was a prosperous man." And it is for this special purpose it is written, "And Joseph saw Ephraim's children of the third generation; the children also of Machir, the son of Manasseh, were brought up on Joseph's knees." Long life, and honoured old age, a quiet grave; these were the blessings reckoned desirable in Jewish modes of thought : and they are mentioned as evidences of Joseph's happiness.

And this, too, is Life. The sorrows of the past stand out most vividly in our recollections, because they are the keenest of our sensations. At the end of a long existence we should probably describe it thus, "few and evil have the days of the years of thy servant been." But the innumerable infinitesimals of happiness that from moment to moment made life sweet and pleasant are forgotten; and very richly has our Father mixed the materials of these with the homeliest actions and domesticities of existence. See two men meeting together in the streets;

mere **acquaintances**. They will not be five minutes together
before a smile will overspread their countenances, or a merry
laugh ring of, at the lowest, amusement. This has God done.
God created the smile and the laugh, as well as the sigh and the
tear. The aspect of this life is stern, very stern. It is a very
superficial account of it which slurs over its grave mystery, and
refuses to hear its low, deep undertone of anguish. But there
is enough, from hour to hour, of bright, sunny happiness, to
remind us that its Creator's highest name is Love.

Now turn to the spirit of Joseph's inner life. First of all,
that life was forgiveness. You cannot but have remarked that,
conversant as his experience was with human treachery, no
expressions of bitterness escape from him. No sentimental
wailing over the cruelty of relations, the falseness of friendship,
or the ingratitude of the world. No rancorous outburst of
misanthropy : no sarcastic scepticism of man's integrity or
woman's honour. He meets all bravely, with calm, meek,
and dignified forbearance. If ever man had cause for such
doubts, he had ; yet his heart was never soured. At last, after
his father's death, his brothers, apprehending his resentful recollections of their early cruelty, come to deprecate his revenge.
Very touching is his reply. " Fear not : for am I in the place
of God ? But as for you, ye thought evil against me : but God
meant it unto good, to bring to pass, as it is this day, to save
much people alive. Now therefore, fear ye not : I will nourish
you and your little ones."

This is the Christian spirit before the Christian times.
Christ was in Joseph's heart, though not definitely in Joseph's
creed. The Eternal Word whispered in the souls of men

before it spoke articulately aloud in the Incarnation. It was the Divine Thought before it became the Divine Expression.* It was the Light that lighteth every man that cometh into the world, before it blazed into the Day-spring from on high which visited us. The Mind of Christ, the Spirit of the years yet future, blended itself with life before He came; for His words were the Eternal Verities of our humanity. In all ages love is the truth of life. Men cannot injure us except so far as they exasperate us to forget ourselves. No man is really dishonoured except by his own act. Calumny, injustice, ingratitude—the only harm these can do us is by making us bitter, or rancorous, or gloomy; by shutting our hearts or souring our affections. We rob them of their power if they only leave us more sweet and forgiving than before. And this is the only true victory. We win by love. Love transmutes all curses, and forces them to rain down in blessings. Out of the jealousy of his brothers Joseph extracted the spirit of forgiveness. Out of Potiphar's weak injustice, and out of the machinations of disappointed passion, he created an opportunity of learning meekness. Our enemies become unconsciously our best friends, when their slanders deepen in us heavenlier graces. Let them do their worst; they only give us the Godlike victory of forgiving them.

2. Distinguished from the outward circumstances, we find simplicity of character : partly in the willingness to acknowledge his shepherd father in Egypt, where the pastoral life was an abomination ; partly in that incidental notice which we have

---

* Λόγος ἐνδιάθετος—προφορικὸς.

of the feast at which he entertained his brethren, where the Egyptians sat at a table by themselves and Joseph by himself. So that, elevated as he was, his heart remained Hebrew still. He had contracted a splendid alliance, by marrying into one of the noblest families in Egypt, that of Potipherah the priest of On. And yet he had not forgotten his country, nor sought to be naturalized there. His heart was in that far land where he had fed his father's flocks in his simple, genial boyhood. The divining cup of Egyptian silver was on his table; but he remembered the days when the only splendour he knew was that coat of many colours which was made for him by his father. He bore a simple, unsophisticated heart amidst the pomp of an Egyptian court.

There is a great mistake made on the subject of simplicity. There is one simplicity of circumstances; another simplicity of heart. These two must not be confounded. It is common to talk of the humble poor man, and the proud rich man. Let not these ideas be inseparably blended together. There is many a man who sits down to a meal of bread and milk on a wooden table, whose heart is as proud as the proudest whose birth is royal; there is many a one whose voice is heard in the public meeting, loudly descanting on legal tyranny and aristocratic insolence, who in his own narrow circle is as much a tyrant as any oppressor who ever disgraced the throne. And there is many a man who sits down to daily pomp, to whom gold and silver are but as brass and tin, and who bears in the midst of it all a meek, simple spirit, and a "heart refrained as a weaned child"; many a man who lives surrounded with homage, and hearing the applause and flattery of men perpetually, on whose heart these things fall flat and dead, without raising one single emotion of fluttered vanity.

The world cannot understand this. They cannot believe that Joseph can be humble, while he is conscious of such elevation above the crowd of men, not even dreaming of it. They cannot understand how carelessly these outsides of life can be worn, and how they fall off like the unregarded and habitual dress of daily life. They cannot know how the spirit of the cross can crucify the world, make grandeur painful, and calm the soul with a vision of the Eternal Beauty. They cannot dream how His life and death, once felt as the grandest, write mockery on all else, and fill the soul with an ambition which is above the world. It is not the unjewelled finger : nor the affectation of an almost quakerish simplicity of attire : nor the pedestrian mode of travelling : nor the scanty meal : that constitute humility. It is that simple, inner life of real greatness, which is indifferent to magnificence, and, surrounded by it all, lives far away in the distant country of a Father's Home, with the cross borne silently and self sacrificingly in the heart of hearts.

3. One characteristic of Joseph's inner life remains— benevolence. It was manifested in the generosity with which he entertained his brethren, and in the discriminating tenderness with which he provided his best beloved brother's feast with extraordinary delicacies. These were traits of thoughtfulness. But farther still. The prophetic insight of Joseph enabled him to foresee the approach of famine. He took measures accordingly ; and when the famine came, the royal storehouses were opened, and every man in Egypt owed

his life to the benevolent providence of the Hebrew stranger.
It was productive of a great social revolution. It brought, by
degrees, all the land of Egypt into the power of the crown, so
that a kind of feudal system was established, every man
holding in direct tenancy from the crown. Hence the nation
became compacted into a new unity, and power was concen-
trated in the hands of government, partly by the pecuniary
revenue thus added, and partly by the lustre of goodness
which Joseph had thrown round the royal acts. For acts like
these are the real bulwarks of a throne. One such man as
Joseph does more to strengthen the crown than all the
speculations, solemn or trifling, which were ever written on the
"divine right of kings." There *is* a right divine which
requires no elaborate theory to make it felt.

II. The death of Joseph was in accordance with his life.

1. The funeral was a homage paid to goodness. Little is
said in the text of Joseph's funeral. To know what it was, we
must turn to the earlier part of the chapter, where that of
Jacob is mentioned. A mourning of seventy days; a funeral
whose imposing greatness astonished the Canaanites, they
said, "This is a grievous mourning to the Egyptians."
Seventy days were the time, or nearly so, fixed by custom for a
royal funeral; and Jacob was so honoured, not for his own
sake, but because he was Joseph's father. We cannot suppose
that Joseph's own obsequies were on a scale less grand.

Now, weigh what is implied in this. This was not the
homage paid to talent, nor to wealth, nor to birth. Joseph was
a foreign slave, raised to eminence by the simple power of

goodness. Every man in Egypt felt, at his death, that he had lost a friend. There were thousands whose tears would fall when they recounted the preservation of lives dear to them in the years of famine, and felt that they owed those lives to Joseph. Grateful Egypt mourned the Good Foreigner; and, for once, the honours of this world were given to the graces of another.

2. We collect from this, besides, a hint of the resurrection of the body. The Egyptian mode of sepulture was embalming; and the Hebrews, too, attached much importance to the body after death. Joseph commanded his countrymen to preserve his bones to take away with them. In this we detect that unmistakable human craving, not only for immortality, but immortality associated with a form. No doubt, the Egyptian feeling was carried out absurdly. They tried to redeem from the worm the very aspect that had been worn, the very features they had loved; and there was a kind of feeling that, while that mummy lasted, the man had not yet perished from earth. They expected that, in process of years, it would again be animated by its spirit.

Now Christianity does not disappoint, but rather meets, that feeling. It grants all that the materialist, and all that the spiritualist, have a right to ask. It grants to the materialist, by the doctrine of the resurrection of the body, that future life shall be associated with a material form. Leaving untouched all the questions which may be raised about the identity of the atoms that have been buried, it simply pronounces that the spirit shall have a body. It grants to the spiritualist all he ought to wish, that the spirit shall be free from evil. For it is a mistake of ultra spiritualism to connect degradation with the thought of a risen body ; or to suppose that a mind, unbound by the limitations of space, is a more spiritual idea of resurrection than the other.

The opposite to spirituality is not materialism, but sin. The form of matter does not degrade. For what is this world itself but the form of Deity, whereby the manifoldness of His mind and beauty manifests, and wherein it clothes itself? It is idle to say that spirit can exist apart from form. We do not know that it can. Perhaps even the Eternal Himself is more closely bound to His works than our philosophical systems have conceived. Perhaps matter is only a mode of thought. At all events, all that we know or can know of mind exists in union with form. The resurrection of the body is the Christian verity, which meets and satisfies those cravings of the ancient Egyptian mind, that expressed themselves in the process of embalming, and the religious reverence felt for the very bones of the departed by the Hebrews.

Finally, in the last will and testament of Joseph we find faith. He commanded his brethren, and through them his nation, to carry his bones with them when they migrated to Canaan. In the Epistle to the Hebrews that is reckoned an evidence of faith. " By faith Joseph gave commandment concerning his bones." How did he know that his people would ever quit Egypt? We reply, by faith. Not faith in a written word, for Joseph had no Bible ; rather, faith in that conviction of his own heart which is itself the substantial evidence of faith. For religious faith ever dreams of something higher, more beautiful, more perfect, than the state of

.hings with which it feels itself surrounded. Ever, a day future lies before it ; the evidence for which is its own hope. Abraham, by that creative faith, saw the day of Christ, and was glad. Joseph saw his family in prosperity, even in affluence ; but he felt that this was not their rest. A higher life than that of affluence, a nobler destiny than that of stagnant rest, there must be for them in the future ; else all the anticipations of a purer earth, and a holier world, which imagination bodied forth within his soul, were empty dreams, not the intuitions of God's Spirit. It was this idea of perfection, which was "the substance of things hoped for," that carried him far beyond the period of his own death, and made him feel himself a partaker of his nation's blessed future.

And that is the evidence of immortality. When the coffin is lowered into the grave, and the dull, heavy sound of earth falling on it is heard, there are some to whom that sound seems but an echo of their worst anticipations ; seems but to reverberate the idea of decay for ever, in the words, " Earth to earth, ashes to ashes, dust to dust." There are others, to whom it sounds pregnant with the expectations of immortality, the " sure and certain hope of a resurrection to eternal life." The difference between these two feelings is measured by the difference of lives. They whose life is low and earthly, how can they believe in aught beyond the grave, when nothing of that life which is eternal has yet stirred within them? They who have lived as Joseph lived, just in proportion to their purity and their unselfishness, must believe it. They cannot but believe it. The eternal existence is already pulsing in their veins ; the life of trust and high hope, and sublime longings after perfection, with which the decay of the frame has nothing at all to do. That is gone—yes—but it was not that life in which they lived; and when it finished, what had that ruin to do with the destruction of the Immortal?

For what is our proof of immortality? Not the analogies of nature; the resurrection of nature from a winter grave, or the emancipation of the butterfly. Not even the testimony to the fact of risen dead; for who does not know how shadowy and unsubstantial these intellectual proofs become in unspiritual frames of mind? No, the life of the spirit is the evidence. Heaven begun is the living proof that makes the heaven to come credible. "Christ in you" is "the hope of glory." It is the eagle eye of faith which penetrates the grave, and sees far into the tranquil things of death. He alone can believe in immortality who feels the resurrection in him already.

There is a special application to be made of this subject to our hearts. It is not often that the pulpit can be used for a funeral eulogium. Where Christ is to be exalted in solitary pre-eminence, it is but rarely that the praise of man may be heard. Rank, royalty itself could not command from the lips of a minister of the King of kings one syllable of adulatory, undeserved, or unfelt homage. But there are cases in which to loftiness of birth is added dignity of character; and then we gladly relax the rule, to pay a willing tribute to the majesty of goodness.

There is one to whom your thoughts must have reverted often during the history which we have been going through, suggesting a parallel, all the more delicately felt from the absence of direct allusion. That royal Lady, for whose loss the marvellous uniformity of the unbroken funeral hue which pervades this congregation tells eloquently of general mourning, came to this land a few years ago, like Joseph, a foreigner. Like Joseph, the earlier years of her sojourn were spent in comparative obscurity. Like Joseph, she had her share of calumny, though in a different form. There are many here who can remember that in that year when our political feuds had attained the acme of rancour, the irreverent lip of party slander dared to breathe its rank venom upon the name of one of the gentlest that ever adorned a throne. There are some who know how that unpopularity was met : with meekness—with Christian forgiveness—with quiet dignity—with that composure which is the highest result and evidence of strength. Like Joseph, she passed through the temptations of a court with unsullied spotlessness ; like Joseph, the domestic and social relationships were sustained with beautiful fidelity ; like Joseph, she lived down opposition, outlived calumny ; like Joseph, she used the noble income entrusted to her, in acts of almost unexampled munificence ; like Joseph, her life was chequered with sorrow, and when the clouds of earlier difficulties had cleared away, the rainbow sign of peace, even in the midst of broken health, spanned the calmness of her evening years ; like Joseph, she will have a regal burial, and her ashes will repose with the dust of England's princes, amidst the mourning of the nation in which she found a home.

The homage which is given to her is not the homage yielded to rank, or wealth, or genius. There will be silver on her coffin, and magnificence in the pageantry which attends her to the grave ; but it is not in these that the glory of her funeral lies.* These were the privileges of the most profligate of her ancestors as well as her. These are the world's rewards for those whom she delights to honour. There will be something in her funeral, beside which these things are mean. There is a grandeur in a nation's tears ; and they will be shed in unfeigned reverence over the remains of a'l that was most queenly, and all that was most womanly. No political fervour mixes with her obsequies. She stood identified with no party politics ; no peculiar religious party mourns its patroness. Of all our jarring religious sects, in the Church, and out of it, not one dares to claim her as its own. Her spirit soared above these things. It is known that she scarcely recognised them. All was lost in the sublimer name of Christian. It is a *Christian* who has passed from this earth away, to take her place in the general Assembly and Church of the firstborn : to stand before God, the Judge of all, among the spirits of the just made perfect.

One word more. Honouring the Queen, profoundly reverencing the Woman, let not contemplation stop there. Do not bury thought in the human and finite. Mildly as her lustre shone on earth, remember it was but one feeble ray of the Light that is Uncreated. All that she had she received. If we honour her, it is to adore Him who made her what she was. Of His fulness she had received, and grace for grace. What she was she became through adoring faith in Christ. It

---

* This anticipation has not been realized. In one of the most touching and unaffected documents that ever went right home to English hearts, the Queen of a British Sovereign requested to be borne to the grave as the wife of a sailor.

P

is an elevating thing to gaze on human excellence, because
through it the Highest becomes conceivable. It is a spirit-
stirring thing to see saintly goodness asserting its celestial
origin by turning pale the lustre of the highest earthly rank.
For in this universal mourning our noble country has not
bowed the knee in reverence to the majesty which is of time.
Every heart in England has felt that the Sovereign was merged
in the servant of Christ. "The king's daughter was all
glorious within." Hers was *Christian* goodness. Her eyes
had beheld the King in His beauty, and therefore her life was
beautiful, and feminine, and meek, and simple. It was all
derived beauty. She had robed herself in Christ. "Reflecting
back, as from a burnished mirror, the glory of the Lord, she
was changed into the same image, from glory to glory, even as
by the Spirit of the Lord." *

SUBJOINED are the directions given by her late Majesty for her own
funeral. The reader will be glad to have them preserved in a form less
inconvenient than the columns of a newspaper. Should he be one who feels
it a relief to miss, for once, the worn-out conventionalisms of religious
expression, and come in contact with something fresh and living, he will
find more in these quiet lines than in ten sermons ; more to make a very
happy tear start ; more of the simplicity and the beauty of the life in God ;
more to cool the feverishness of his heart, and still its worldliness into
silence ; more of that deep rest into which the meek and humble enter;
more that will make him long to be simple and inartificial, and real, as
Christ was, desiring only, in life and death, and judgment, to be found in
HIM.

---

* 2 Cor. iii. 18. This appears to be the true force and rendering of the
metaphor.

[Copy.]

" I die in all humility, knowing well that we are all alike before the Throne of God, and request therefore that my mortal remains be conveyed to the grave without any pomp or state. They are to be moved to St. George's Chapel, Windsor, where I request to have as private and quiet a funeral as possible.

" I particularly desire not to be laid out in state, and the funeral to take place by daylight, no procession, the coffin to be carried by sailors to the chapel.

" All those of my friends and relations, to a limited number, who wish to attend, may do so. My nephew, Prince Edward of Saxe Weimar, Lords Howe and Denbigh, the Hon. William Ashley, Mr. Wood, Sir Andrew Barnard, and Sir. D. Davis, with my dressers, and those of my ladies who may wish to attend.

" I die in peace, and wish to be carried to the tomb in peace, and free from the vanities and the pomp of this world.

" I request not to be dissected, nor embalmed ; and desire to give as little trouble as possible.

(Signed)   " ADELAIDE R.

" November, 1849."

PRINTED BY

SPOTTISWOODE AND CO. LTD., NEW-STREET SQUARE

LONDON